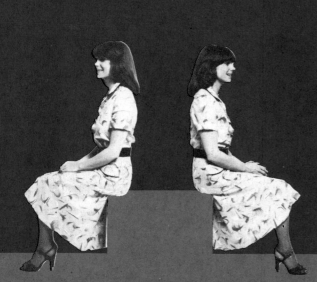

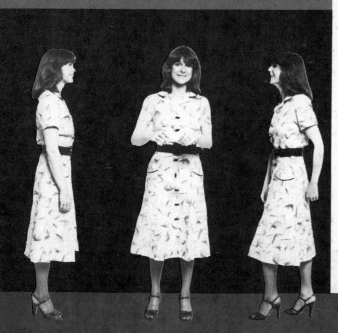

Biddy Baxter, Edward Barnes & John Adcock devised and wrote the Blue Peter Book

CONTENTS

MARK
ROSS

Hello There!

And what a year it's been! – There's scarcely room in this 16th Blue Peter Book to write about all the news, but we've done our best to record the highlights.

The biggest excitement of all was undoubtedly our 20th Birthday celebrations, and our grand reunion of past Blue Peter presenters which ended with our nationwide Balloon Release.

One thousand four hundred and seventy-eight programmes is an awful lot of television, and twenty years is a record time for a programme like Blue Peter to run non-stop. If you'd been watching the first ever programme in 1958, you could be viewing the 1979 editions with your own children!

One interesting development is the number of Blue Peter viewers who are now helping us as experts. David Langford, for instance, who directed our Birthday Blue Peter, appeared on the very first programme as a guest when he was 14 years old. Schoolboy Brian Banks, who brought his pet tree frogs to the studio and who is now at University studying biology, has joined us as our fish expert; and in 1967 when 10-year-old Jeremy Sams came to the studio to sing carols with his school, little did we know that he'd return 12 years later to play for us as a fully qualified musician. Just a few of the Blue Peter badge winners who are making names for themselves.

Last spring, after almost seven years on the programme, Lesley decided she wanted to spend more time at her home in the country with her husband Terry, who has Multiple Sclerosis. It was a sad moment for all of us, but we were delighted to welcome Tina as the newest member of the Blue Peter team.

Tina was hardly a stranger – after playing the part of 12-year-old Lizzie Dripping in the popular BBC series, she was a familiar face to lots of viewers. You can find out how she became an actress and joined Blue Peter on page 70.

Do you recognise any of these photographs? They've all been in Blue Peter. Turn to page 76 for the answers.

Our other new girl, Goldie, fully deserves her place on the cover of our 16th Book. She's grown into a beautiful and well-behaved (well, nearly always!) Golden Retriever, and we were very proud when she was invited to take part in the Personality Parade at the world's most famous dog show – Cruft's. You can catch up on her training on pages 10–13.

The death of poor old Freda was the saddest blow of the year. She died in her hibernation box last April – of natural causes – according to the Senior Veterinary Officer of the London Zoo. She was between 25 and 30 years old, and as European tortoises have a life span of approximately

20 years, she'd had a good innings! Our new tortoises, Maggie and Jim, made their first appearance on Election Day and they seem to have taken to life on TV!

If you sent stamps for our Medi-Bikes, there's news of our Appeal on page 57. Thanks to you, we were able to provide over 1000 Medi-Bikes to help save the lives of babies and little children in Tanzania. Not only that – spurred on by your efforts, the Government lent a hand too – so we were able to send £60,000 worth of medical supplies as well as the bikes. A marvellous start to the International Year of the Child.

The great thing about the Blue Peter Appeals is that every little not only helps – it mounts up in a colossal way. Let us know what good cause you'd like us to support for our next Appeal – we'd like to hear from you!

Jim

Maggie

Lesley Judd

Simon Groom

Chris Wenner

Tina Heath

Jill

Jack

Goldie

4

5

8

9

10

RVW 909M

GB

5

THE DAY I CLIMBED ABOARD

There used to be a tradition on Blue Peter that the new boy never made his first entrance by sitting on that horse-shoe seat and being introduced – "This is . . . . who's come to join us."

No. Before Tina arrived every one slipped in through the back door. John Noakes, for instance, was a fresh-faced young lad who was taking a ski lesson from Valerie on a new dry-ski practice slope at the National Recreation Centre at Crystal Palace. Peter Purves arrived at the same place by giving life-saving lessons to John and Valerie in the Olympic Pool. Lesley was teaching the boys go-go dancing, and Simon taught Lesley how to be a disc jockey. It was always the last item in the programme, and there was something in the way the "stranger" said "goodbye" that made the discerning viewer raise an eyebrow and say "I wonder . . . ?"

All this was explained to me after I had done my audition and been told that I'd got the job. And then came the frightening question.

"What can *you* do?"

As soon as someone asks me a question like that my mind goes a complete blank.
"Er. . . Ride a bicycle?"
"Not very spectacular."
"Speak Swedish? My mother is a Swede."
"Not desperately athletic."
"Swim?"
"Peter did that . . !"
And then it came to me.
"I can water-ski –"
"Great!" they said. "We'll do it next Friday."

I was telling the truth, but I hadn't done it for ages. My father's jobs took him to a series of very hot, faraway places with strange-sounding names like El Salvador, and I used to spend my holidays from school swimming and water-skiing.

There were two problems: a) it was a long time ago, and b) the water temperature in El Salvador was about 20 degrees C. It was now October – in England – and I don't think anyone dared measure the temperature of the water on the lake that had been chosen for my début. The man who invented the wet suit has my everlasting gratitude. Without that I would have died of exposure before I said my first "Hello".

But I soon got used to the water – and to my intense relief I found I was still able to water-ski. It's rather like riding a bicycle – once you've done it, you never quite forget it.

I was just beginning to get my confidence back when Simon and Lesley arrived with the Blue Peter film crew. Simon had never done water-skiing before – the idea was for me to teach him – but as this was to be *my* first experience of filming, I don't know which of us was the most scared!

I think it might have been me. Actually, I think I was too cold to have any emotions at all. The trouble about learning a water sport is that you have to spend a great deal of time up to your neck in water, whilst your instructor on the boat tells you what you're doing wrong.

"Now relax, Simon – just relax. You were doing fine at the beginning – then you started stiffening . . . "

"Started stiffening," I thought it was rigor mortis setting in. Actually, Chris was a terrific instructor. He seemed to know just when I needed encouragement – and when to correct me from going wrong.

I just couldn't seem to get up on the water – and for a while I thought I might become the world's first subaqua skier.

"Bring your knees upward – let your skis come up – arms slightly bent. That's it – that's it! Skis right in the water and away you go!"

I was up! I really was water-skiing. It was the most marvellous sensation. I should have thought of something telling to say to camera – but all that came out was "Wheeeah!"

7

I was an absolutely marvellous water-skier – on land! Chris took me very patiently through all the moves on the shore, and said I was a very good pupil. But when I saw Simon being dragged under water a couple of times, I decided that someone had better look after Goldie – and that someone was going to be me!

After my lesson, I joined Lesley on the bank to watch Chris having a go at ski-jumping. He was on the other side of the lake, almost out of sight. We heard a sudden roar as the boat opened up and Chris disappeared behind the great wall of water thrown up by his skis, as he headed towards us at breathless speed.

He swung out across the wake of the boat and began to line himself up with the jump. There was a harsh scrape as his skis hit the ramp a split second before he sailed through the air to make a perfect landing on the water. Then he glided with nonchalant ease across the lake until he stopped within a couple of feet of where we were sitting on the bank. It was enough to make you spit!

The last bit was something I'd seen people doing in El Salvador, but I'd never actually attempted myself. The idea is to strap on an 8ft (2.5 metre)-wide kite to your back and belt along on skis behind the boat until you take off.

Lesley, Simon and Goldie climbed into the towing boat with the Blue Peter cameraman. As the boat began to gather speed I hoped I wasn't going to make my first and last appearance on John Craven's Newsround. "New Blue Peter man dies before he starts!"

When we got up to about 35 mph, I began to feel the water offering less and less resistance as the kite began to tug at my shoulder straps – and I was airborne. The boat with Lesley and Simon was suddenly below me! I was so thunderstruck, I couldn't even manage a "Wheeah!" for the camera. That was partly because I was remembering the old adage – "What goes up must come down" – and I hadn't really worked out how that was going to be achieved!

After flying the length of the lake the boat began to slow down – and I began to descend. The slower you come down, the more chance you have of staying elegantly upright. A really fast descent ends up at the bottom of the lake. I thought I was doing it beautifully until the last three feet – then I lost concentration for a second, and the next thing I knew was the waters of the lake closing over my head.

I bobbed up again in a second and the boat circled round with Lesley and Simon offering a helping hand, whilst Goldie barked excitedly.

"Come on – in you get!" said Lesley. So I scrambled aboard – to join Blue Peter.

good as Goldie

It was a proud moment when Goldie and I stood alone in the arena of the world's most famous dog show. Goldie had been invited to take part in the Personality Parade at Cruft's, and we were in the company of such renowned Top Dogs as Prince Charles' *Sandringham Harvey,* Air Dog *Zimba,* and Search Rescue Dogs *Jan* and *Zeb.*

We only stood on our own for a short while, but it seemed like hours as the commentator spoke glowingly about Goldie and praised Blue Peter for all the programme had done on behalf of dogs. The roar of applause from the twenty-thousand strong spectators was a humbling experience and I hoped Goldie would behave herself! She did – good old Goldie came up trumps and remembered her training as she walked smartly to heel. Her concentration was what one would expect of a well-brought-up Golden Retriever – not even the slightest tug on the lead as we walked past handsome Champion *Harrowhill Huntsman* – Cruft's Best in Show winner 1978.

Thank goodness all those sessions in the Blue Peter studio and

Training out of doors – in Hampstead, London.

Steps are a huge hurdle for a small puppy.

Hampstead Heath, my London home and my parent's farm at Dethick, had paid off. And we ended up with two of the coveted Personality Parade rosettes – one for Goldie and one for Blue Peter.

Like all dogs, the motto for training Goldie has been "a little and often". The important thing to remember is that training takes *time* and there are no short cuts.

One advantage with Golden Retrievers is that they're working dogs and they really do want to learn. Goldie became house-trained when she was about

Goldie quickly became accustomed to the roar of traffic and bustle of crowds.

10 weeks old, and if she ever makes a mistake nowadays, it's generally my fault for not giving her a run at the strategic moment.

Walking to heel, coming when she's called and retrieving, are all things we've worked hard at during the past year and she's mastered them very well indeed. As well as at home and in the studio, we've trained out of doors, and Hampstead has been an ideal place for getting Goldie used to the roar of traffic and the bustle of crowds. But before setting off for an outdoor training session, I always gave her collar one last check to make sure it was fitting properly – with space for no more than two fingers underneath. The last thing you want is for your pup to slip her collar when you're out in heavy traffic.

Goldie started learning to retrieve in the Blue Peter studio.

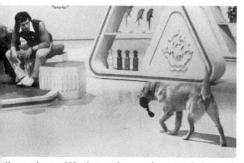  

When she sniffed out the sock containing a lump of cheese, we gave her lots of praise.

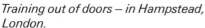

Thirteen weeks old *and Goldie*
20 lbs 12 oz (9.40 kg)

Seven months old *and Goldie posed to have her portrait painted when Rolf Harris visited the studio.*

I took Goldie on to the Heath or into the countryside for her training *off* the lead. Only when we were well away from any roads was she allowed to run free, and before the serious training, I always gave her a good run to let off steam. It's hard work getting a dog's attention, but gradually Goldie learned to concentrate and stayed with me when I walked – even when I changed my direction.

Goldie's retrieving lessons started with me putting some kind of juicy titbit in an old sock and throwing it fairly short distances at first. As Goldie tried to sniff it out, I encouraged her and was very firm with my commands to get her to bring the sock back to me. She had to learn to sit at my feet and then give up the sock without growling or barking back. And as

Golden Retrievers are very possessive dogs, this wasn't easy.

I gradually threw the sock further and further away so that she had to do a great deal of searching before she found it. Just as sheep dogs will round up sheep, even if they've never seen them before, a retriever will search and sniff and fetch things instinctively. But all the time you have to praise your pup, and make the whole session seem like a game. At the end of the training, your dog should finish up doing exactly what you told him, *and* have enjoyed himself!

Goldie's certainly enjoyed her training and so have I. She's growing into the sort of dog you can take anywhere and be proud of.

She's so gentle, she never growls

or snaps, even when she's surrounded by enormous crowds, and she really does enjoy meeting people.

Goldie's scored a great hit with celebrities like Mike Oldfield and famous film stars like Yul Brynner and Virginia McKenna. She's come face to face with chimpanzees, swans, a sea lion, and even a 90-strong Welsh Male Voice choir – without so much as a snarl – *and* had her portrait painted by Rolf Harris into the bargain!

Does this all sound too good to be true? Well, of course, Goldie has her lapses – mostly to do with food. She finds it hard to resist a tasty smell, but I think Jack and Jill have forgiven her for almost demolishing their third birthday cake before they'd had a bite!

26 March 1979: *Goldie celebrated her first birthday (one day late!) with her mother and father and her six brothers and sisters – and Derek Freeman, the Guide Dogs for the Blind Puppy Walking Manager, who chose her for us.*

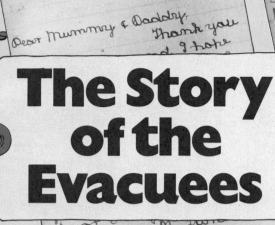

sept. 1st

Dear Mummy & Daddy,
Thank you
... I hope

... when I am
go's ... ...
We have had two or mo...
Raids in fact more I am
sure. The "All clear" has
... what a short they
... passed but they were
... ts and lots of them
oh dear!. No more
news.
love Jill

I do NOT CRY

Hitler

Do not worry
about him

floor ...
top of us. M ...
sleeping there too.
... I go down to
the farm nearly all the

The Story of the Evacuees

I DO NOT CRY

THEY WALKED THROUGH THE STREETS TO THE RAILWAY STATION. EVERYONE THOUGHT THE ENEMY WOULD ATTACK WITH POISON GAS, SO THEY ALL CARRIED A GAS MASK, IN A SQUARE CARDBOARD BOX.

EVERYONE HAD A LABEL TIED ON, LIKE A PIECE OF LUGGAGE, SO THAT NO ONE WOULD GET LOST.

MANY OF THE FATHERS WERE GOING AWAY TO JOIN THE ARMY, NAVY OR AIR FORCE. NO ONE KNEW WHEN THEY WOULD MEET AGAIN.

On a Sunday morning, just over forty years ago, the wailing cry of a siren howled over London. It was the first Air Raid warning of the war.

It was 3 September 1939. Britain and Germany were at war, and the war was to last for nearly six years.

In fact, that air raid warning was a false alarm, but everyone was certain that waves of bombing aircraft would come, raining death out of the skies.

The greatest danger would lie in the big cities, so the government planned to clear the towns as soon as war started. All the children were to be sent away. The scheme was called the Evacuation – and the children were called the EVACUEES.

Plans were made and rehearsals carried out, and when the war really started, everyone knew what to do.

THE MOTHERS WAVED GOODBYE AND SMILED CHEERFULLY, BEFORE THEY WENT BACK TO THEIR SILENT EMPTY HOUSES,

THE CHILDREN TRIED TO BE CHEERFUL TOO, EVACUATION WAS A BIG ADVENTURE,

WHEN THE TRAIN STARTED, HOME SEEMED A LONG WAY AWAY,

THE JOURNEY TOOK HOURS, AND WHEN THEY ARRIVED THE LITTLE ONES WERE ALMOST TOO TIRED TO REMEMBER THEIR OWN NAMES,

MANY OF THEM SPENT THE NIGHT IN MAKESHIFT HOSTELS, WAITING TO BE TOLD WHERE TO GO,

AT LAST EVERY EVACUEE WAS ALLOCATED TO A HOSTESS – THEY WERE ALL VERY DOUBTFUL OF EACH OTHER,

All schoolchildren in big towns like London, Birmingham or Manchester, that were likely targets in air raids, went with their teachers to the nearest railway station. Special trains carried them away to quiet places in the country, where it was hoped they would be safe.

They had to say goodbye to their parents and their homes and their pets, and go to places they had never seen before. When they arrived, tired out with travelling, officials met them and sent them to strange homes where they were to be looked after. Sometimes the lady of the house was kind and welcoming – sometimes she hated the idea of having strange children in her home. Some of the children had never left home before and they were shy and frightened. Some of them had never been well looked after and they were dirty and rough.

Most people tried very hard to settle down and get on together. The evacuees tried to be good, and big brothers and sisters looked after the little ones. They wrote cheerful letters to their parents, not saying how much they missed them. "Don't you know there's a war on?" was the catchphrase everyone repeated if someone grumbled.

But often they were very homesick. School was difficult, too, because the evacuated school had to double up with a school in the new place, sharing the buildings and playgrounds. It made things hard for everybody.

For nearly a year after war broke out, there were no air raids over Britain. The government knew they would come, and begged the parents to leave the children in their new homes in safety – but the children were homesick and their mothers were lonely.

No one minded the threat of danger nearly so much, if only they could be together again. So many children went back to the cities, and when the air raids really came, they lived through them bravely alongside their families.

At last the last air raid was over – and the war came to an end, but no one, parents or children, teachers, the "aunties" in the country, ever forgot the evacuation and the experiences they had all shared together.

LUCKY EVACUEES WHO HAD BEEN SENT TO THE SEASIDE TRIED TO PRETEND IT WAS ALL A HOLIDAY.

TOWN CHILDREN WHO HAD NEVER BEEN IN THE COUNTRY BEFORE WERE TAKEN BLACKBERRYING BY THEIR HOSTESSES.

SOME HOSTESSES WERE ABSOLUTELY AMAZED BY THE STRANGE CHILDREN.

THE RAILWAYS RAN SPECIAL TRAINS TO BRING THE MOTHERS AND FATHERS TO SEE THE CHILDREN, AND THE EVACUEES WAITED LONGINGLY FOR THEM.

IT WAS A MARVELLOUS MOMENT WHEN THEY ACTUALLY ARRIVED.

WHEN THE WAR WAS OVER, KING GEORGE VI, OUR PRESENT QUEEN'S FATHER, SENT A SPECIAL MESSAGE TO ALL THE BOYS AND GIRLS IN BRITAIN.

8th June, 1946

TO-DAY, AS WE CELEBRATE VICTORY, I send this personal message to you and all other boys and girls at school. For you have shared in the hardships and dangers of a total war and you have shared no less in the triumph of the Allied Nations.

I know you will always feel proud to belong to a country which was capable of such supreme effort; proud, too, of parents and elder brothers and sisters who by their courage, endurance and enterprise brought victory. May these qualities be yours as you grow up and join in the common effort to establish among the nations of the world unity and peace.

George R.I

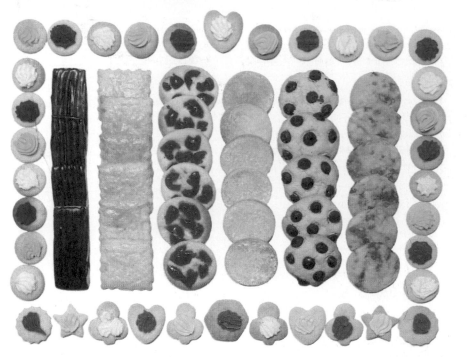

No such luxury as these for the evacuees during the Second World War – they'd have taken a whole week's ration of butter and sugar! But by 1979 standards it's an economical recipe and the results are delicious!

Use the basic recipe and add your favourite flavouring. These biscuits make good presents for Mums and Dads, Aunts, Uncles and Grandads – as well as Grannies. Put them in a decorated jar for an extra special touch.

Granny's Biscuits

Variations on Basic Recipe

Cherry, Coconut and Squashed fly Biscuits
Mix cherries, coconut or currants with flour and sugar before adding lemon and egg.

Candy Kisses
Mix a little icing sugar with some water, add a few drops of colouring, and put small dots in the middle of the biscuits.

Chocolate Chip Biscuits
Make small balls of mixture and push in chocolate chip pieces before cooking.

Basic Recipe

200g
or
8oz } self-raising flour

100g
or
4oz } castor sugar

100g
or
4oz } butter or margarine

1 egg (beaten)

Rind and juice of half a lemon

Pinch of salt

1 Mix flour, sugar and salt in a basin. Rub in butter or margarine until the mixture resembles breadcrumbs.

2 Add grated rind and juice of half a lemon and beaten egg. Mix to a stiff paste.

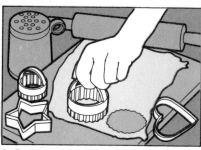

3 Roll out thinly on a well-floured board. Cut into circles.

4 Place on greased baking sheet and cook in moderate oven at 160 degrees C/235 degrees F, Gas mark 3 for about 15 – 20 minutes, until pale golden.

Chocolate Finger Biscuits
Melt an ordinary bar of chocolate and spread it over biscuits (cut out in oblong shapes)

Coffee Cream Sandwich
Sandwich two biscuits together with icing made from
50 g or 2 oz butter
100 g or 4 oz icing sugar
Teaspoonful of instant coffee dissolved in a few drops of hot water.

Jars
Decorate your jars with pictures cut from cards or magazines, coloured sticky tape, or shapes cut from sticky-backed plastic or wallpaper. Paint the lids with enamel paint.

HAPPY BIRTHDAY
OR 1478 PROGRAMMES LATER.....

Our magnificent Twentieth Birthday cake was created by BBC Pastry Chef, Ted FitzMaurice.

How *do* you celebrate one thousand four hundred and seventy-eight Blue Peters? We decided on a grand Birthday reunion with all the Presenters – past and present – a Birthday Quiz and a Birthday Balloon Release. Mix them together and the result was a day that will stick in our memories for ever!

There were two colossal coincidences that got us off to a good start. Coincidence number one was that our 20th Birthday actually fell on Monday 16 October 1978 – twenty years to the *day* from the very first transmission in 1958.

The second was that on 16 October 1958, a 14-year-old boy was a guest on the programme. He was actor and dancer David Langford, who was a famous child star. From the age of 12 David had been a well-known TV face. He'd danced in ballets, taken leading parts in operas, and had appeared in dozens of plays. His guest appearance on the first-ever Blue Peter was something of a scoop for the programme, and he helped to demonstrate some conjuring tricks

Little did David know – or anyone else for that matter – that twenty years later he would be sitting in the Control Gallery of Television Centre's Studio 8, directing Blue Peter's Twentieth Birthday Programme! Or that he'd make history by becoming the first Blue Peter viewer ever to direct the programme.

David Langford – the boy who appeared on the very first Blue Peter.

Our celebrations began two weeks *before* our Birthday when we held our Birthday Quiz. The idea was that the winners would be invited to Television Centre so that Blue Peter viewers would actually be able to join in the Studio celebrations. There were three Quiz questions: "How many pets has Blue Peter had?" (The answer was ten – Petra, Jason, two parrots - Joey & Barney - Freda, Patch, Shep, Jack, Jill and Goldie, and we *didn't* count the twenty goldfish in our Italian Sunken Garden, because we hadn't given them names.)

The second question was: "How many Appeals has Blue Peter held?" (And the answer was nineteen.)

Twenty years later, David was behind-the-scenes, directing our Birthday programme.

16 October 1958 – *Christopher Trace and Leila Williams presented the first-ever Blue Peter.*

16 October 1978 – *Chris and Leila back in the studio. Lesley's photo of Leila was taken on the first programme in 1958.*

The final question, which was quite tricky, was:

"How many Blue Peter programmes have there been, up to and including today's?" The answer to that was 1478 – and they included all the "Blue Peter Flies the World" programmes.

Out of all the thousands of entries, only one person got all three answers right, and only thirty-four people sent two out of three correct answers. So to be absolutely fair, we put all those replies in a tombola, gave them a shuffle, and picked two out. Nine-year-old Helen Knight of Dunstable and thirteen-year-old Robert Edmonds of Somerton in Somerset were the lucky winners, and we were delighted to have them with us on the great day, plus the one person who got all three answers correct – fifteen-year-old Richard Merrett of Pinner in Middlesex.

The very first Blue Peters were quite different from what you see today. For a start, the programme only lasted fifteen minutes and it was only transmitted once a week.

The first two Presenters were Christopher Trace and Leila Williams. In those days there were extremely clear divisions between items for boys and items for girls. Chris mostly showed model railways and our present Blue Peter Layout grew out of that early idea. Leila, who won the title Miss Great Britain 1957, did items about dolls. There were no pets, no badges, and no ship symbol – all very different from Blue Peter nowadays. But there *was* the now-familiar Signature Tune called "Barnacle Bill", which Mike Oldfield rearranged for us in 1979.

Chris and Leila both came to our Birthday Reunion and so did Valerie Singleton who joined Blue Peter in 1962. John Noakes was next to take part, followed by Peter Purves and then Lesley. And to complete the Birthday Scene were Blue Peter's new boys – Simon and Chris No. 2 – Christopher Wenner.

As John was filming for his *Go With Noakes* series, he couldn't actually be with us in the flesh. But he came as a cardboard cut-out and

In 1962, Valerie Singleton took over from Leila. The programme's pets were Petra and Jason, the Sealpoint Siamese.

recorded a special message on film, which we played into the programme.

What with the thousands of birthday cards, the Chalk Farm Band of the Salvation Army playing Happy Birthday, and the enormous Birthday cake – complete with twenty candles – made by the BBC's Head Pastry Chef, Ted FitzMaurice, we all felt in a party mood. There was so much to talk about, the day flew by, and Derek Kibble, our Floor Manager,

had to be quite fierce to stop all the gossiping when the massed Blue Peter Presenters should have been rehearsing! Most of the conversations began, "Do you remember when . . .", and some very amusing memories were brought back when we showed excerpts from some famous Blue Peter mistakes. Lulu, the baby elephant who wouldn't leave the studio, disgraced herself all over the floor – *and* pulled her keeper down in the

1972. By now John Noakes, Peter Purves and Lesley Judd had joined the team.

mess - was definitely the star attraction. But there was also the magic moment when three BBC firemen made an unexpected appearance on the programme when they dashed into the studio brandishing their fire extinguishers to damp down the Girl Guides' fire that got out of control.

The grand finale was a nationwide balloon release to launch a special badge to commemorate our 20th birthday. The badge was a strictly limited issue – one for every Blue Peter programme so only 1478 were made.

Each balloon had a label, and people who found them and posted the label back to us won the badges.

We chose five regional Launch Sites, and guest celebrities helped us to release the balloons. There was Isla St Clair in Aberdeen, Eddie Waring in Manchester, Bonnie Tyler in Cardiff, and Mary Peters in Belfast. We all dashed up to the roof of the TV Centre in London to let off the balloons for the South – all very exciting on a "live" programme, with no chance to put right any mistakes!

But all went well. Weatherman Bill Giles said we couldn't have had better weather conditions for the Grand Balloon Release and that was well and truly proved by the distances some of the balloons travelled, as you can find out on page 22.

With the last balloon floating off into the sky, our 20th Birthday

programme was over. It had been a memorable day, and at our party afterwards, where we met all the Blue Peter contributors from the past twenty years, we all drank a toast – "Here's to the next twenty years!"

So here's a date to put in your diary – 16 October 1998. We'll be there – even if some of us come in our wheel chairs!

This rhyme gave us a good laugh! Altogether we received thousands of birthday cards which were all displayed in the studio.

Valerie linked our "live" nationwide Balloon Release from Aberdeen, Manchester, Cardiff, Belfast and London

BALLOON RELEASE

We helped to blow up the balloons for London and the South. Altogether 1478 were released, one for each programme

The winning labels from the two balloons that flew the furthest.

Weatherman Bill Giles told us we couldn't have had better weather conditions for the Release. Blue Peter balloons were blown all over Europe and some reached as far as the borders of East Germany.

Brigitte Hussenöder from Markt Erlbach, near Nuremberg, received her prize in the Blue Peter Studio.

Brigitte had never left her village before, so her sight-seeing tour of London was tremendously exciting.

PADDINGTON TAKES A CUT

Story by Michael Bond
illustrated by "Hargreaves"

As the familiar strains of the *Blue Peter – Special Assignment* signature tune came to an end, Paddington switched off the Browns' television receiver and then sat back in his arm-chair with a thoughtful expression on his face.

Paddington liked the Blue Peter Special Assignment films. Over the years, Valerie Singleton, Peter Purves and Lesley Judd had visited so many of the historic towns of Europe that he now felt as though he knew them all even better through seeing them on television than he would have done had he been lucky enough to visit them himself.

The nice thing about the films was that they were so packed with information, no matter how many times you saw them there was always something new to be learnt.

On this particular occasion there had been an item about topiary – the art of clipping shrubs and hedges into fantastic shapes – and although he knew he must have seen it before, somehow or other it suddenly seemed completely fresh.

During her visit to some gardens on the Continent, Lesley had come across a whole area – a kind of "secret garden" – devoted to hedges and shrubs which over the years had been trimmed into all sorts of shapes; geometrical patterns, tables and chairs, not to mention birds and

animals of various kinds. There had even been a bear; and towards the end of the film, through the use of trick photography, Lesley had pretended to have an encounter with an elephant. It wasn't until she'd tried to feed it a bun that some leaves had fallen off its trunk and the secret had been revealed.

In the normal course of events Paddington wasn't the keenest of gardeners, which was probably why the item hadn't caught his attention the first time round. He liked playing with the hosepipe and picking raspberries during the season, but when it came to carrying out day-to-day tasks, like mowing the lawn and keeping the hedges trimmed, he usually managed to find other more important things to do. However, the idea of actually clipping a bush to make it appear like something else struck him as a very interesting one indeed.

After considering the matter for a moment or two, Paddington stood up again. Although Lesley hadn't time to go into all the details of topiary, he felt sure his friend, Mr Gruber, would be able to help.

A few minutes later there was a click from the front door of number thirty-two Windsor Gardens as it closed behind him and he set off in the direction of the market.

Mr Gruber's antique shop in the Portobello Road was a veritable

treasure trove of good things, and apart from all the old furniture, and the copper, silver, brass and china objects which filled it almost to overflowing, the walls themselves were lined shelves containing books on practically every subject under the sun.

Over the years Paddington had consulted Mr Gruber on a good many occasions and sure enough, no sooner had he voiced his latest request, than his friend reached up to a shelf somewhere near the back of the shop and took down a slim volume with a picture of a rather leafy-looking peacock on the jacket.

"I think you'll find all you want to know in here, Mr Brown," he said. "It's called *Clippings from my*

Hedgerow and it's by Ebenezer Hawthorne."

Mr Gruber went on to explain that Mr Hawthorne was very well known in gardening circles for his work with shrubs and that his designs were to be found in some of the best gardens in England.

"But be careful, Mr Brown," he warned, as Paddington made ready

to leave. "Don't forget – what comes off won't always go back on again."

Paddington thanked his friend for his help and advice, and after raising his hat he turned and hurried back in the direction of Windsor Gardens again. He was the sort of bear who believed in striking while the iron was hot and with the sun already well past its peak there was no time to be lost.

To his relief the Browns were nowhere to be seen when he arrived home. Although, by and large, he was allowed a fairly free paw in the garden, from past experience he felt it might be better if he presented them with a finished work rather than try to explain what his intentions were.

He spent some while in the shed poring over his new book, and when he finally emerged carrying Mr Brown's best shears in one paw and a large sheet of paper in the other, there was a determined gleam in his eye.

Mr Hawthorne was nothing if not thorough in his description of how to go about matters, and in the end Paddington had confined himself to making copies of some of the many illustrations which graced the pages of the book. In particular there was a photograph of a large bear which the author had fashioned for his own garden and which was apparently so life-like even his own dog gave it a wide berth.

After making a few passing snips through the air in order to get used to handling the shears, Paddington looked around in search of a suitable subject for his attentions. Most of Mr Brown's shrubs were either of the flowering variety and rather spindly, or they were so short they wouldn't have lent themselves to being shaped into a hedgehog let alone anything on two legs.

Apart from that, according to Ebenezer Hawthorne, far and away the best place for a work of topiary was in the centre of a lawn where it could be seen from all angles, and in the end, much to his disappointment, Paddington had to settle for an old yew bush which was growing alongside the garden fence.

Taking a deep breath, he stood on tip-toe and snipped at one of the topmost twigs.

Almost immediately he regretted his action, for there came a bellow of

rage from the other side of the fence and to his horror the Browns' neighbour, Mr Curry, rose into view clutching his eye.

"Bear!" roared Mr Curry, as he focused his gaze on Paddington. "What are you doing now, bear? Something hit me in the eye just then!"

"It's topiary, Mr Curry," cried Paddington, trying to hide the shears under his duffle-coat. "It was only a twig and I didn't mean it to go over your fence. I didn't know you were spying . . . I mean . . ." He broke off as Mr Curry's face started to change colour.

"*Toe* parings!" bellowed the Browns' neighbour. "How dare you throw toe parings over my fence!"

"Not toe parings, Mr Curry," exclaimed Paddington. "To*piary*. That's quite a different thing. It's to do with cutting shrubs. I'm making a bear . . . look!" And he held his sheet of paper up in the air to show what he meant.

"A bear?" snorted Mr Curry as he peered at Paddington's drawing. "I don't see what you want to make a *bear* for. The place is enough of a bear garden already without making it worse."

"Oh, I can do lots of other things, Mr Curry," said Paddington confidently. "Peacocks, elephants, kangaroos . . ." His face fell. "The only trouble is I haven't got any proper bushes to work on."

Mr Curry grabbed the piece of paper and stared at it. "I didn't know you went in for this sort of thing, bear," he growled.

"Bears are good at cutting things, Mr Curry," said Paddington, waving his shears in the air again.

"Hmm. Yes . . . well . . . watch what you're doing." Mr Curry stepped back a pace and eyed Paddington thoughtfully. "I wouldn't mind a bit of topiary in *my* garden," he continued. "A peacock in the middle of the lawn might raise the tone a bit, and it just so happens that I have a bush that needs pruning.

"Mind you," the Browns' neighbour looked round to make sure no one else was listening and then beckoned Paddington to come closer. "I wouldn't want every Tom, Dick and Harry to have one. I'd like mine to be exclusive. If I had one that was exclusive it's quite possible I might not mention your trying to poke my eye out with a stick just now."

"Oh, I'm sure yours would be exclusive, Mr Curry," said Paddington, anxious to make amends. "I'd make sure yours would be like nothing that had ever been done before."

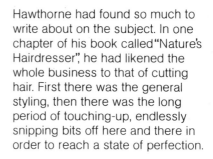

"Hmm." Mr Curry came to a decision. "In that case, bear," he said, lifting some boards in the fence to one side, "you can start right away. I shall leave you to it while I go out and get some ointment for my eye before the shops close."

Paddington needed no second bidding and a few moments later, almost before the sound of Mr Curry's side gate being slammed shut had died away, he was hard at work.

At first sight, Mr Curry's bush had all the signs of being a very promising model to work on indeed. Apart from the fact that it was ideally situated in the middle of the lawn it had been untouched for so long it was positively crying out for someone to give it a trim.

Paddington consulted his drawing several times to get the feel of things and then made the first few cuts. It was really very satisfying and he could quite see why Mr

Hawthorne had found so much to write about on the subject. In one chapter of his book called "Nature's Hairdresser", he had likened the whole business to that of cutting hair. First there was the general styling, then there was the long period of touching-up, endlessly snipping bits off here and there in order to reach a state of perfection.

In the case of Mr Curry's bush the general styling was over in no time at all. In fact, had he been there to see it, even the Browns' neighbour would have been hard put to find fault. Really and truly, although it might not have taken in another peacock who happened to be passing, the end result did bear a striking resemblance to the one shown on the front of Mr Gruber's book.

It was when Paddington turned his attention to the final touching up process that he began to experience trouble. Another of Mr Hawthorne's hobby horses was the care one had to take in order to avoid upsetting the balance of nature. In Paddington's case it wasn't so much nature itself he was worried about, it was the balance of Mr Curry's peacock. No sooner had he snipped a piece off one side than he found he had to snip a piece off the other.

Gradually the pile of clippings by his side grew larger and larger, but it wasn't until he stood up and moved back a few paces to view the end result that he realised with a start just how much he *had* taken off.

Paddington gazed mournfully at what was left of Mr Curry's bush. Any resemblance it once might have had to a bird had long since gone. Even allowing for the failing light, it was

definitely more pea than cock. In fact, not to put too fine a point on it, there was little more than a stump left in the ground, and even Mr Hawthorne himself would have found it difficult to fashion more than a bedraggled sparrow out of the remains, let alone anything larger.

Paddington sat down and peered hopefully at his book, but as if to rub salt into his wound, almost the first words he read were the ominous ones: "Some of the simpler shapes can be completed in as short a time as ten years."

"Ten *years*!" exclaimed Paddington, addressing the world in general as the book fell from his paws.

From the expression on his face in the accompanying illustration, Mr Hawthorne obviously thought that even that length of time was pretty good going, but equally obvious was the fact that he'd been living in balmier days, untroubled by next-door neighbours like Mr Curry. As far as Paddington was concerned any solution to his problem which took more than ten minutes was cause for alarm, and as even that amount of time began to dwindle away, his face grew longer and longer.

Although he'd promised the Browns' neighbour that his bush would end up looking like no one else's, Paddington had a nasty feeling Mr Curry would be far from happy with the result, and by now there were so many twigs and branches lying on the ground the chances of glueing them back together in anything like the right order seemed very remote indeed.

In the past, Paddington had often found that when things were at their very worst something often happened to make them come right again; almost as if, like Mr Hawthorne's belief in the balance of nature, some unseen force came to the rescue in order to tip the scales in the opposite direction, and it was as he gazed around Mr Curry's garden that a gleam of hope suddenly came into his eyes.

The Browns' neighbour had obviously recently taken delivery of something big, for beside his dustbin there was a large pile of white packing material. The sight of it reminded Paddington of an item he'd seen a few weeks before on Blue Peter, an item which at the time he'd found very interesting, but for one reason or another had never followed up.

He scrambled to his feet. Desperate situations demanded desperate measures, and with Mr Curry already overdue from his visit to the chemist there wasn't a moment to lose. Soon, the only sound which broke the silence was that of heavy breathing intermingled with a strange squeaking sound as Paddington set to work again.

Mr Curry gazed approvingly at the result of Paddington's labours. "I must say I take my hat off to you, bear," he said grudgingly. "That peacock is one of the best I've ever seen outside of a zoo.

"In fact," he continued, with a sudden burst of generosity, "if you come and see me tomorrow I might even give you five-pence for your trouble."

"Thank you very much, Mr Curry," said Paddington gratefully. "Perhaps you'd like to give it to me now?" he added hopefully. "You might not want to in the morning."

The Browns' neighbour glared at Paddington through the gathering dusk. "Nonsense, bear!" he growled, banging his hand on the top of the bush in order to emphasise his words. "Why shouldn't I want to? If I say I'm going to do a thing I do it. Are you suggesting I'm the sort of person who goes back on his word? Why I'll have you know . . . . "

Whatever else Mr Curry had been about to say was lost for all time as he brought his hand down again and suddenly encountered empty air.

Turning round, he gazed disbelievingly at the spot where, a moment before, the peacock had stood, and then at the sight of it bouncing across the lawn, shedding leaves and branches as it gathered speed and headed towards the fence.

"Bear!" he bellowed, when he found his voice at last. "Come back, bear!"

But he was too late. Paddington was already fleeing from the scene. There was a momentary pause by the fence as he scrambled to get both himself and the bird through the gap at the same time, and then he disappeared from view.

Five-pence or no five-pence, quite clearly Mr Hawthorne had lost one of his readers for the rest of that day, if not for all time.

"Lots of you will probably remember," said Lesley, as she turned to face the camera, "that a few weeks ago we did an item on carving polystyrene – the material which turns up as packing in practically everything you buy these days and which always seems to end up being thrown out for the dustmen.

"A lot of you sent in pictures of the things you made after the programme . . . cars, trains . . . there was even a model of the Television Centre here in Wood Lane, but today we've got something really special to show you."

As the camera zoomed out to a wider shot, Lesley stood up and strolled across to a rostrum where a large and impressive-looking green object was on display.

"It's a peacock . . . carved entirely by paw and decorated with real leaves. I'm afraid some of them have dried out under the heat of the studio lights, but it's so unusual we felt sure you'd like to meet the owner so we've asked him along to the studio today . . ."

"Good Heavens!"

"Paddington!"

A cry of amazement went up from the Brown household as the Director cut away to another picture and the familiar figure of Paddington appeared on their screen.

"No wonder that bear wanted us to watch Blue Peter," said Mrs Bird. "I had a feeling he had something up his sleeve."

"And what's he doing with a peacock?" said Jonathan. "I didn't know he even liked birds."

"Shh!" broke in Judy. "Lesley's telling us."

The Browns fell silent as Lesley guided Paddington through the various stages of his model; how he had carved the peacock out of several pieces of polystyrene tied together, and how he'd then covered it by pushing leaves and twigs from Mr Curry's bush into the material.

"I must say it was very kind of Mr Curry to let you do all that," said Lesley.

"Well, he didn't actually *let* me, Miss Judd," admitted Paddington. "It was a bit of a surprise. It sort of happened."

"Oh, Lord," groaned Mr Brown. "Here we go again."

"Quiet, Henry," broke in Mrs Brown. "We don't want to miss anything."

"Talking of things which have happened," said Lesley, turning to face the camera, "we have a surprise here in the studio now. We all thought Paddington's model was such a good idea we decided to

make one for ourselves. In fact, we've gone one better – with the aid of a few bits and pieces from the Blue Peter garden we've made one that's actually alive."

"Mercy me!" Mrs Bird nearly dropped her knitting as the picture on their screen changed yet again. "If that's not Paddington it's his double."

The Browns sat glued to their seats as the camera, which had started by showing a wide shot of the studio, moved steadily in towards a gaily coloured object standing apart from all the rest. From a distance it looked remarkably like Paddington, but as it began to fill the screen they could see that is was almost entirely covered with flowers.

"You see," said Lesley, as she talked over the picture for the benefit of the viewers at home, "what we've done is take Paddington's idea a stage further. We've made large holes all over the model we built of him and we've filled them with pots of flowers . . . blue ones for the duffle-coat . . . dark, almost black pansies for the hat . . . and brown foliage for the fur. We've even . . ." Lesley paused in order to allow the Director to cut to a close-up of an orange-coloured jar,

"we've even used marigolds for the marmalade pot."

"Now," she asked, as the rest of the team joined her in sitting alongside Paddington ready to close the show, "what do you think of that?

"Or, perhaps more to the point," she added, "what are you going to do with it?"

Oblivious of the studio manager making frantic wind-up signs alongside the camera taking his picture, Paddington considered the matter very carefully before replying. When he'd taken his model of the peacock along to the Blue Peter offices he'd had no idea quite so many things would happen and he wanted to make sure he did the right thing.

"I think," he announced at last, much to everyone's relief, "I shall give it to Mr and Mrs Brown's next-door neighbour. I promised him he would have something unique, and I don't think even Mr Curry could grumble when he sees what I've brought him."

EVERYTHING IN THE GARDEN'S LOVELY

30 March. Cutting the first sod.

Spring 1978: Our gardening expert, Percy Thrower, had spent four years showing us how to grow vegetables and flowers in a small, 3.5 metre x 3.5 metre patch of ground, and he thought it was time for us to be a bit more adventurous. His suggestion was to create an Italian sunken garden next door to the vegetable patch. It was a huge undertaking, and one that was going to take us three months to complete . . .

Digging a trench for the pond's drainag

Tea break!

Danger! Men (and woman!) at work!

After all our hard work, vandals wrecked the site. What a stupid and pointless thing to do.

20 April. The garden is sunk and the pond is dug.

Just seven days later: the walls are built and the pool lined with concrete.

Treasure! Digging deep we discovered this tile and bottle from an exhibition that was held on this site 71 years ago.

The first of 3 tons of crazy paving is laid.

Simon joined Blue Peter just in time to make a great impression.

All our hand and footprints – even the animals put their best feet forward!

Final touches: fixing the plaque . . .

. . . filling the pond . . .

. . . and putting in the 150 plants.

Last of all, Brian Banks gave us expert advice on what kind of fish to put in the pond. They were: 13 Goldfish, 6 Golden rudd and 1 Golden tench.

EVERYTHING IN THE GARDEN'S LOVELY

For Percy Thrower our Italian sunken garden is a triumph. All of us at the BBC who sit out on a warm sunny day and eat our sandwiches, can't thank him enough.

I'M DREAMING OF A WHITE GARDEN

Television producers do have some peculiar ideas. Take Alan Russell, producer of **Record Breakers** and the **All Star Record Breakers Christmas Spectacular**. Alan asked us if he could use our Italian Sunken Garden for one of the scenes in his Christmas show. Naturally we agreed, but we were a little taken aback when he said he wanted our garden covered in snow!

Now, television programmes have to be planned weeks in advance, and it doesn't snow much in early December in London. So as Alan couldn't depend on the weather to provide snow – he called in a fire engine! I met Ted Grumpt who explained that the fire engine was full of foam and he was to spray it all over the garden.

There were strange things to be done before Ted could start spraying. The pond was covered over, and huge net curtains hung on the adjacent brick wall. While all this was happening, the stars – our old friends Roy Castle and Peter Purves – were rehearsing. They were hardly recognisable dressed as eskimos.

A Television Producer's igloo – made of wood!

Ted's fire engine's full of foam – television snow!

Netting covered our garden ready to be sprayed with snow.

Producer Alan Russell rehearsing his stars, Roy Castle and Peter Purves.

With Ted and me ready to spray on the "snow", the set was cleared, I turned on the nozzle and thick white foam gushed from the hose. In no time at all, our Italian Sunken Garden looked like the North Pole. There was even an igloo – but made of wood, not ice! Cameras had been brought from Studio 8, and after a couple of rehearsals, the shout went up! "Quiet please – this is a take."

"Run VT."

"Five, four, three, two, one . . . "

Peter began singing "Gone Fishing . . . in Percy's Italian Garden", while Roy played the mellophonium and Chris, Simon and I, all dressed as Eskimos, sat fishing and adding the odd Record-Breaking remark. Even Goldie joined in, although she didn't look much like a Husky!

"All right everybody, that was a good one!" came the call. That meant Alan was happy. He'd recorded his snow scene.

Now all that was left was to get rid of the snow, and a hosepipe and plenty of water did the trick. The foam disappeared and our Sunken Garden was back to normal!

Hundreds of gallons of foam . . .

. . . start to cover everything!

"Action!" Roy plays the mellophonium, Peter sings *Gone Fishin'* and Simon and Chris become Eskimos for the day.

Plane Tree.

THE TRADESCANT TRUST

Acacia Tree.

The Gardening Family

Lilac.

Tradescantia.

Tulip Tree.

John Tradescant (Father)

John Tradescant (son)

John Tradescant (grandson)

Every garden in Britain is fairly certain to have some of these plants growing in it. They were all brought to this country by one family – the great gardening family of Tradescant.

Gladioli.

Virginia Creeper.

Michaelmas Daisy.

1 The first John Tradescant was born when Elizabeth I was queen. He became gardener to Lord Salisbury, one of the most important men in the kingdom, with a fine house at Hatfield. John Tradescant was sent to France to buy rare plants – he came back with oleanders, myrtles, figs, oranges and aubergines – as well as 206 cypress trees.

2 Lord Salisbury wanted a stream in his garden, paved with coloured pebbles and sea shells, so in Paris John Tradescant bought a chest of pebbles and six boxes of shells.

3 He was not only a gardener, but a very knowledgeable botanist. He went to Archangel, in Russia – the first botanist who had ever been there – and saw larch trees growing.

4 Two years later, he went to North Africa and saw gladioli growing. "Many acres of ground spread over with them," he said. He brought back some bulbs to England.

5 Then he became chief gardener to Queen Henrietta Maria. She had been a French princess, so she was called the Rose and Lily Queen, because she united the Rose of England with the Lily of France. John Tradescant's official title was "Keeper of His Majesty's Garden, Vines & Silkworms" at Oatlands Palace, and he was in charge of the Great Garden, the Long Garden, the King's Privy Garden, the Queen's Privy Garden, and the New Garden, with an arched walk 100 yards long and 476 fruit trees.

6 Now he was doing so well, John Tradescant bought a house at Lambeth, across the River Thames from Westminster, and only reached by ferry. He made a splendid garden with all his new discoveries, and friends and fellow gardeners came to see him. He sold plants, but he was very generous, and often gave seeds and cuttings to enthusiasts. His son, John, was just as interested in the plants as he was himself.

7 When he grew up, young John became a collector and traveller, too. He made three voyages to America and brought back plants unknown in Britain – Virginia creeper, tulip trees, acacia, plane trees, lilac and michaelmas daisies. And he discovered a strange plant that was called after him – Tradescantia.

8 Though plants interested them both more than anything else, the two Johns collected other things too. They set them up in a room they called the Closet of Varieties. People came from far and wide to see their strange things. They called their house Tradescant's Ark, and it was the first public museum in London.

9 One visitor described it all: "They have gathered together beasts, fowl, fishes, serpents, worms (real, though dead and dried), precious stones, coins, shells and feathers – a man might behold in one place more curiosities than he should see if he spent all his life in travel." When old John died, his son took over his work and his house and museum.

10 He had a son of his own, who was called John, as well. He was just as keen on plants as his father and grandfather, and they both hoped he would follow in their footsteps. But unfortunately, he died when he was young, and the Tradescant family died out.

11 A powerful and ambitious neighbour called Elias Ashmole persuaded the family to give him all the curiosities. He used them to start a famous Museum that was called after him – the Ashmolean Museum at Oxford.

12 The three Tradescants – father, son and grandson – were buried in a fine tomb decorated with carvings of trees and plants, shells and stones and monsters – all strange things from the world of nature that fascinated all three of them so much. A verse carved on the tomb tells their story.

"Know, Stranger, ere thou pass, beneath this stone
Lie John Tradescant, grandsire, father, son;
The last died in his spring; the other two
Lived till they had travelled Art and Nature through.
These famous antiquarians that had been,
Both, gardeners to the Rose and Lily Queen,
Transplanted now themselves, sleep here, and when
Angels shall with their trumpets waken men
And fire shall purge the world, these hence shall rise
And change this garden for a Paradise."

The tomb is in St Mary's churchyard, Lambeth, very near the place where the Tradescants had their museum and garden. For years it was forgotten and neglected, but now the Tradescant Trust have made a new, beautiful garden there, to keep the memory of the gardening family green for ever.

Custard Pies

No panto's complete without a bit of slapstick (like Widow Twankey pulling sausages out of her mangle, or Baron Hard-Up in Cinderella using his kitchen floor as a giant pastry board). But nothing quite matches a gooey custard pie for the most spectacular effect of all!

The secret lies in making a mixture that partly sprays out when it hits the actor in the face, yet also sticks to the face at the same time. And if you think any kind of mixture will do – you're wrong! There's a great art in making a good stage Custard Pie.

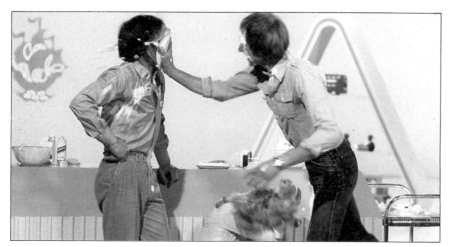

If *you're* putting on a show this Christmas, here's the best recipe we know. It was invented by a friend of ours who worked on the *Crackerjack* programme, and apart from its Spray Power and Stay Power, all the ingredients are perfectly harmless – if you're unlucky enough to get an eye or an ear full – although they're definitely *not* recommended for eating.

Crackerjack Custard Pie

Stale sponge flan cases
Powdered pudding mixed with a little milk
Powdered artificial cream and a small amount of aerosol shaving foam.

Mix the topping until it's medium thick. Pile into the flan cases and "decorate" with shaving foam.
Whip the pudding and pile into the flan case.
Whip the powdered cream until it's quite stiff and pour on top, adding small blobs of shaving cream for decoration.
Put the pie on to a paper plate – and serve!

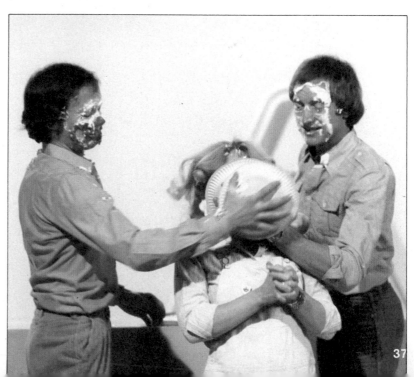

Phil Roberson who designed our Blue Peter studio set.

BLUE PETER STUDIO

Margaret Parnell who adapted Phil's design and created this model.

Have you ever wanted to be a television director? If so, here's your chance! Build your very own Blue Peter studio, with exact scale models of our shelf units, seats and ship, as well as all the cameras, microphone booms and lights.

With this perfect replica, you can have Blue Peter in your home any time of the day or night! So budding directors, first take a large grocery box . . .

Studio

Cut away one long side of the grocery box. Cover the inside with pale grey card, or white card painted grey. (That's because our studio walls are grey – we cover up the grey with a white curtain called the cyclorama.) Cut a long piece of white card about 4 cm lower than the studio sides and long enough to cover all three sides. Glue to the middle of the back and bend the card so it curves round the sides of the studio. Trim so that it ends 10 cm from the edges of the box. When the studio is finished, you could make several of these cycloramas, all different colours, and paper clip them over the white one. This will give the studio a "Top of the Pops" look.

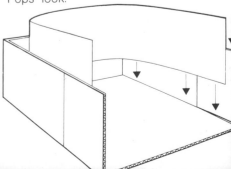

Materials

Here's everything else you'll need:
Thin cream card: Stiff card (any colour); paint in grey, green, black, light brown & cream; thin round black elastic; strong glue; 6 mm and 12 mm dowelling; 1 x 50 ml toothpaste packet; 1 x 85 ml toothpaste packet; meatcube box; 6 small black beads; 2 brass paper fasteners; green felt; scrap of woodgrain sticky-backed plastic; felt-tipped pens or paints to colour; cork; ball-point pen refill (the plastic kind); aluminium kitchen foil; fuse wire; stiff wire; 1 drinking straw; button approx. 2–2·5 cm diameter; washing-up liquid bottle top; sticky tape; matchbox; snap fasteners; black cotton, tracing paper.

Figures

Turn to the front and end of this book for exact scale pictures of us, Goldie, Jack, Jill, Maggie and Jim. Trace these onto card, colour and cut out. Make a criss-cross stand for each figure. For the animals, a thin piece of card glued to the back and bent makes an easy stand.

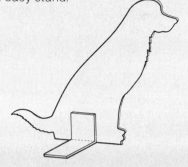
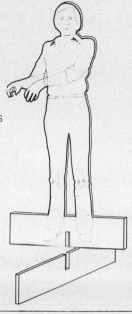

Shelf

There are six shelf units in the Blue Peter studio, but you can make as many or as few as you like. Trace round the shelf twice on thin cream card and cut out. Snip black lines at the corners. Score and fold front of shelf back along dotted lines.

Cut a strip of card 39 cm x 2 cm and glue round the sides of the shelf unit. When dry, glue the back of the unit to the strip. Cut lengths of stiff card for shelves. Bend ends down and glue inside shelf unit.

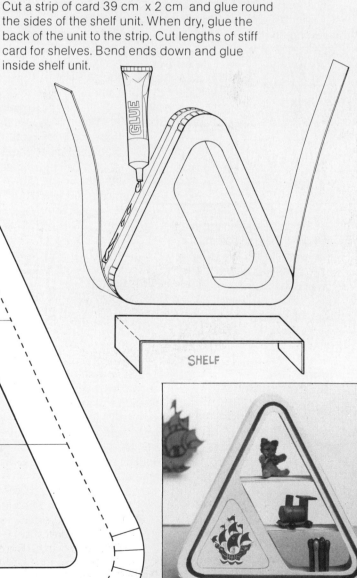

SHELF LEVEL

CUT OUT THIS AREA

SHELF LEVEL

GLUE

SHELF

TV Camera

Normally we use five cameras in the studio, though occasionally we've had a sixth hand-held lightweight camera. Trace onto thin card. Cut out and score along dotted lines. Make hole at ● and thread 0.5 metre of thin black elastic through to inside and tie knot. Cut through thick black lines marked X. Glue A under B, C under D, E under F. Cut off the cap from a plastic washing-up bottle top and glue to underside of camera.

View finder Trace and cut out. Score dotted lines. Glue G under H. Paint black. Glue K to K on camera.

Lens Hood Trace and cut out. Score dotted lines. Glue I under J. Paint black and glue sloping parts of the lens hood inside X on the camera.

Pedestal Trace and cut in stiff card. Take remaining part of bottle top you used to make camera and push the part that fits into the bottle into the cut out circle.

Stand Trace and cut out from stiff card. Glue on piece of 12mm dowelling 5.5 cm long to centre of base. Paint all matt grey. Fix camera onto pedestal by pressing cap into place on bottle top and put the top onto the stand (M on N). If the camera doesn't move freely, sandpaper the top of the stand.

Microphone boom

Whenever you watch Blue Peter and we're in the studio, there's always a microphone just out of shot at the top of the picture (it has been known to be in shot, too!). The "mike" is fixed on the end of a telescopic boom, which the operator can move in and out by a series of pulleys. We only use one or two "booms", depending on how complicated the programme is.

Base Trace and cut out Fig. 1 from stiff card. Cut out centre hole and small hole for cable to thread through. Make three wheels by cutting 5 mm wide sections from a piece of 12 mm dowelling. Glue wheels to base where marked.

Platform Trace and cut out Fig. 2 in stiff card. Make holes where marked. Push the end of a 7–8 cm long piece of stiff wire through hole in button and twist to secure. Cover the top of the button to look like a seat. Bend the other end of wire in shape as shown in Fig. 3. Push end of wire through one of the small holes in platform. Bend wire flat on the card and cover with sticky tape to hold it in place. Cut a second platform shape, this time omitting the hole made for the wire. Glue both platform pieces together matching up the holes and sandwiching the end of wire between the two parts.

Post For centre post cut off a 13 cm long piece of 6 mm dowelling. Glue base in place 1 cm from end and platform in place 4 cm from base. Wind a piece of sticky-tape round dowelling under platform and base to prevent them slipping down. For the mike cable, glue one end of a 60 cm length of thin round black elastic near top of post, thread the other end through the small holes in platform and base.

Boom Cut off a 12 cm length of drinking straw. Put a piece of sticky-tape across the middle of straw with ends of tape down the sides of post. Wind a second piece of tape at top of post to cover ends of first piece of tape and end of elastic.

Paint grey all over except wheels and tape holding straw at the top which should be painted black.

Cover a ball-point pen refill, the plastic kind, with aluminium kitchen foil. Twist some fuse wire into microphone shape winding the ends round tip of refill. Push other end of refill into straw putting on a dab of glue if necessary to hold it. Finish off by glueing on small snap-fasteners and pieces of black cotton for wheels and wires.

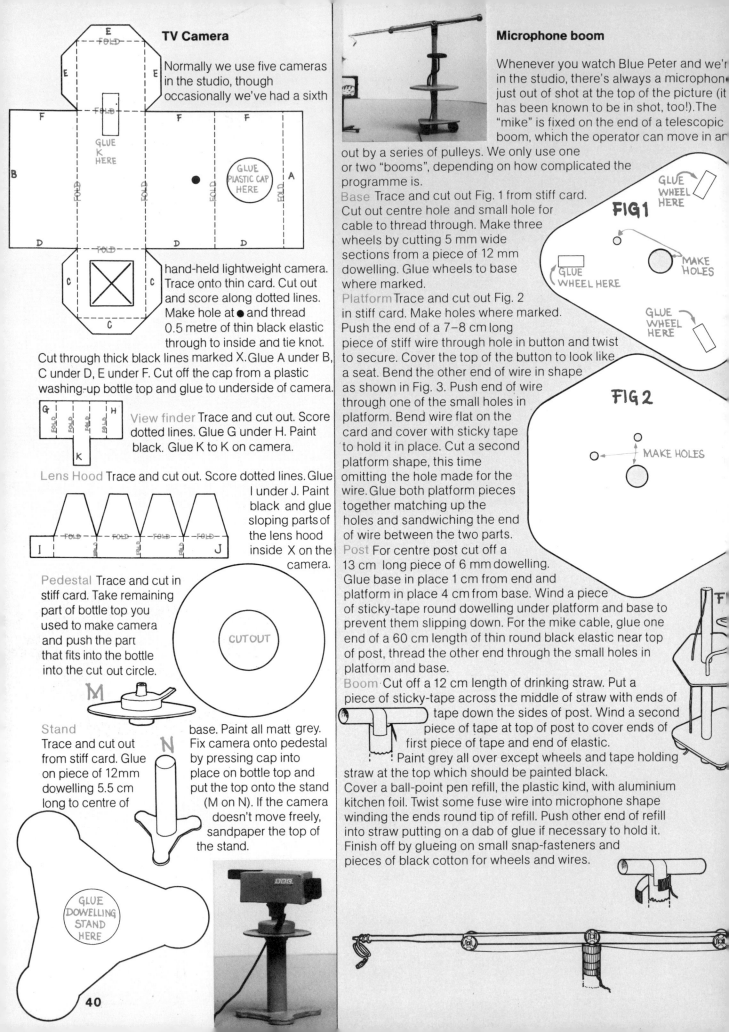

Seating Unit

Trace and cut out seat unit base from stiff card. Colour floor light brown with a cream colour edge. Cut off 5 cm from each end of a 50 ml size toothpaste carton and glue on base where marked, the cut ends of carton towards the middle. Glue strips of cream card right round cartons including the open part at the back. Cut a piece of stiff card to fit over seating. Cover one side with green felt or material, glueing edges onto wrong side of card. Glue in place. For the side seats trace off A twice for top and bottom of side seats, and B for sides, on cream, thin card. Cut out and score along dotted lines.

Fold over on dotted lines. Glue sides to bottom and top, matching Xs and glueing C under D. Paint top green and glue on to seat base where marked 1. Make the second stand slightly higher by cutting the strip for sides 0.5 cm deeper. Make up as before and glue on part of seat unit marked 2.
The hexagon shaped stands dotted around the studio are made in exactly the same way, just alter the depth of the side strips to make stands of various heights.

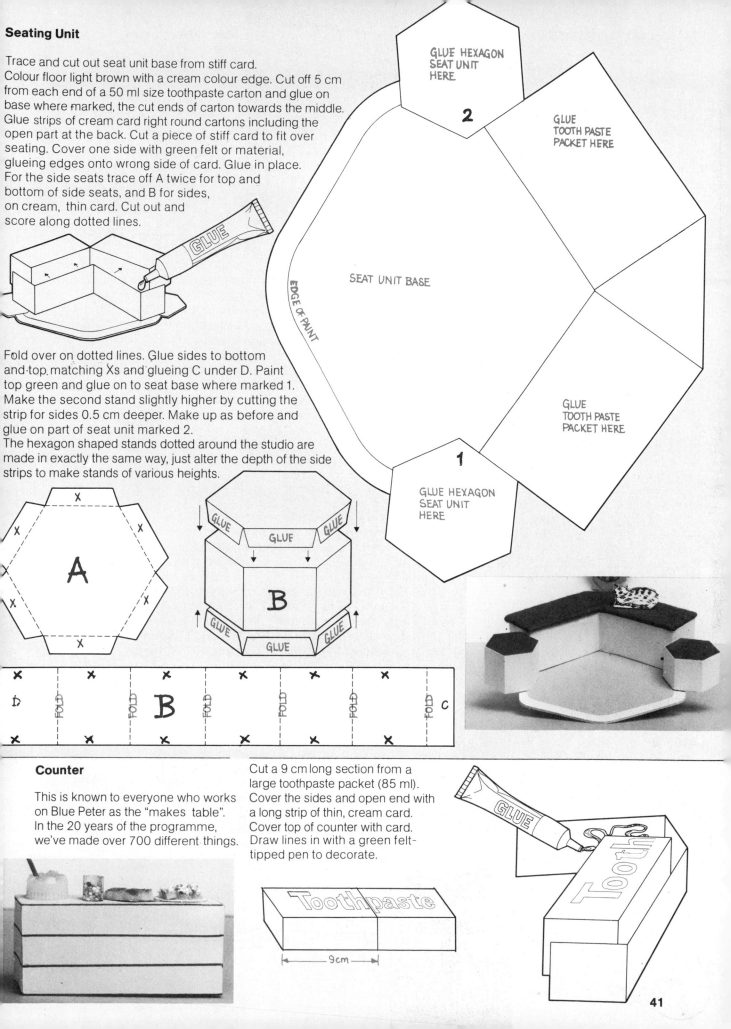

GLUE HEXAGON SEAT UNIT HERE

2

GLUE TOOTH PASTE PACKET HERE

SEAT UNIT BASE

EDGE OF PAINT

GLUE TOOTH PASTE PACKET HERE

1

GLUE HEXAGON SEAT UNIT HERE

A

B

GLUE

GLUE

GLUE

B

GLUE

GLUE

GLUE

D FOLD FOLD B FOLD FOLD FOLD FOLD C

Counter

This is known to everyone who works on Blue Peter as the "makes table". In the 20 years of the programme, we've made over 700 different things.

Cut a 9 cm long section from a large toothpaste packet (85 ml). Cover the sides and open end with a long strip of thin, cream card. Cover top of counter with card. Draw lines in with a green felt-tipped pen to decorate.

Toothpaste

9cm

GLUE

Tooth

41

Cat and Dog Pens

When Jack and Jill and Goldie are not in front of the cameras, they've got their own pens where they can rest, away from the hot studio lights.

Jack and Jill's Pen

Cut off 4 cm from the top of remaining part of toothpaste packet. For the window, cut away all of one side except for a frame round the edge. Glue a piece of clear plastic inside this frame. The open end of

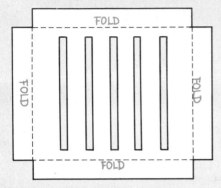

box becomes the top of the pen, so fill this in with a piece of card cut the same size, plus small flaps at edges. Cut slits in card for airholes. Glue flaps over edges of box. Cover sides with cream card except for window. Cut a doorway in one side by just cutting three sides and leaving the fourth for a hinge. Use a brass paper fastener for a door handle.

Goldie's Pen

This is made from a meat cube box. Cut away one large side of box to make the open top. Make a window in another large side, as for cat pen. Cover inside and out with cream card. Make door as for cat pen. Put in a scrap of woollen material for a dog blanket. Use small plastic bottle tops for cat and dog bowls.

Lights

There are 250 lamps in the roof of the Blue Peter studio – they're all on electric hoists, so they can be positioned precisely where the lighting supervisor wants them. We don't suggest you make them all but, here's an idea for a dozen or so.

Trace both shapes onto card and cut out. Score along dotted lines. Bend along scored lines to make a box shape. Glue tab A under B and tabs C under D. Make a hole at ●

Thread a 12 cm length of stiff wire through the hole, twisting wire on the inside to prevent it pulling through again. Bend over and glue tabs E under F. Paint black and glue a circle of kitchen foil in the middle for a lamp.

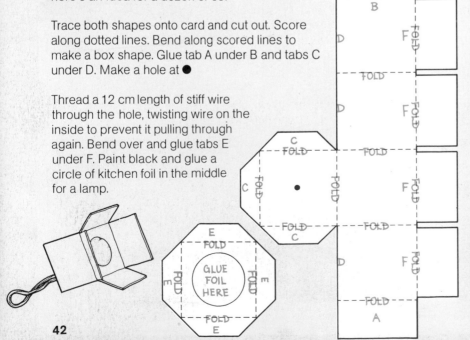

Blue Peter Ship

Our ship is made of blue transparent perspex. We hang it from the studio roof. For our model, though, it's easier to glue it to the cyclorama. Trace the ship onto thin white card and colour blue. Cut out and glue a small piece of cork on the back. Glue the other side of the cork to the back of the studio.

TV Monitor set

There are several of these sets dotted around the studio so that people working on the programme can see the pictures viewers are getting.

Cut a complete matchbox in half and cover with sticky-backed plastic or paint. Draw picture for screen, and glue onto set. Glue small beads at side for control knobs. For top of stand, cut a piece of card slightly bigger than bottom of TV set. Glue on to piece of dowelling, 4 cm long. At other end of dowelling, glue a cross-shaped piece of stiff card. Glue on beads for castors. Paint stand black. When dry, glue set in place with a length of thin, black elastic for cable.

Now with everything made, you're ready for your first production. So stand by cameras, stand by lights, stand by sound. Five . . . four . . . three . . . two . . . one . . .
You're on the air!

42

Sticky Habits

When the great paschal candle which symbolises the risen Christ enters the Abbey Church at Buckfast in the first moment of Easter Day, the youngest monk will chant: "Bless, O Lord, this candle, the work of the bees."

It was the bees which took me to Buckfast Abbey – a Benedictine monastery on the edge of Dartmoor – because one of the world's greatest bee experts is a monk in the Order of St Benedict.

St Benedict, who founded the order in 547, really invented monks. He thought it would be a good idea for men who were devoted to God to live together and worship together in a self-sufficient community. They would grow their own food, build their own house, and church. Prayer was to be the centre of their lives, and when they weren't praying, they would work for the glory of God and for the needs of the community.

The individual brothers soon became experts in different skills; the idea spread, and soon there were Benedictine monasteries all over Europe. Today, 1432 years later, I found that the monks in Buckfast Abbey live very similar lives to those their founder laid down. They have a 300-acre farm where they run 400 head of sheep; they own a private school for 128 pupils, and they sell enormous amounts of the famous Buckfast tonic wine. But it's the home-produced honey that brings apiarists from all over the world to consult the famous Brother Adam.

When the hive gets overcrowded half the bees leave in a swarm to form a new colony.

A worker bee foraging for nectar.

I was taken by the Abbot of Buckfast through the garden to meet the great man. He was standing in the middle of a forest of hives, carefully pulling out the combs which were crawling with millions of bees. Over his monk's habit he wore a bee-keeper's veil, but no gloves.
The Abbot and I donned our veils and walked over to join him. Like many other great experts I have met on Blue Peter, Brother Adam didn't have very much to say for himself. He smiled at me from under his veil, but he was clearly absorbed in his bees. He had a "smoker" in his bare hand which he puffed out occasionally at the crawling, seething mass of wings and bodies. I asked him if there was much danger of being stung.

"Not at this time of the year – they're more ferocious in summer when they're taking the nectar from the heather. But," he said, as he puffed his smoker over the combs, "these are very special bees."
"You mean some bees sting more than others?"
He looked up suddenly.
"Oh yes," he said. "The French bee is a great stinger but our bees are very quiet."

An army of workers attend the Queen. She is the only bee that can breed.

Brother Adam's assistant and I cut up the cones ready for the extractor.

He explained that the bees are a closed community like the monks! They all have special jobs in the hive. Some feed the queen – the only bee that is able to produce eggs to ensure continuity of the hive – whilst some make the wax to build the combs ready to receive the nectar brought in by bees who fly for miles over the moor in search of heather. There are guards on the landing place in front of each hive. If a bee from a different hive lands there in error, they will smell it out immediately and see it off, or sting it to death.

I hurried into the monastery to find out how the honey goes from the combs to the pots on the breakfast table.

It appeared that Brother Adam's talents were not confined to breeding bees. He had also invented a great press to squeeze the honey out of the cones. I joined Peter Donovan, Brother Adam's assistant, and helped him to slice the combs out of the frames with a murderous-looking knife. We piled them up like large slabs of toffee, then wrapped them carefully in a huge muslin cloth which holds back the beeswax and only allows the pure honey to pass through. When Peter had checked every fold, he lowered the lid and the press began to squeeze.

Immediately the rich glutinous substance began to flow out into the sink. The smell of honey was everywhere. I could still smell it at the back of my throat three hours later as I was driving back to London. Peter gave me a spoon which I dipped into the vat for my first taste of Buckfast honey. It had that clean, heady taste – like a breath of summer air on Dartmoor.

From the chapel below I could hear the monks beginning to sing the office of compline – one of the seven times a day they gather together to sing the praises of God – and, perhaps, among other things, to thank Him, for the work of the bees.

Then I helped Brother Adam to extract the honey from the cones.

The Buckfast honey was absolutely delicious.

STICK INSECTS

If you live in a flat and pets are forbidden, you certainly wouldn't annoy the neighbours if you kept Stick insects. They don't bark or need taking for walks, and they don't take up lots of room, either. Expert Don Kennedy really had us baffled when he brought part of his collection to the Blue Peter studio. They were so well camouflaged that half the time the camera crew couldn't find them.

There are hundreds of different kinds of Stick insects, including these **Indian** ones. Can you tell the "Sticks" from the twigs? (see page 76 for the answer). They live quite happily at room temperature and eat privet leaves for food. After hatching from a 2 mm egg, the insect grows from 1 cm to 9 cm and has a total life span of about 12 months. An adult lays lots of self-fertile eggs so your stick insect family will end up a giant one! These seemed pretty large to me, but they were midgets compared with the **Australian Queensland Titan** (top picture) – the world's largest Stick insect. Fully extended, it measures a colossal 30 centimetres, nose to tail.

The **Spiny-Backed Stick Insect**, also found in Queensland, is a good deal smaller than the Titan. With its amazing arched back mechanism, it can imitate a scorpion poised ready to sting, but the Spiny Backed is perfectly harmless.

EXPEDITION·USA

DANCING WITH A BROLLY - A TRADITIONAL FEATURE OF A NEW ORLEANS JAZZ FESTIVAL, AND A MUST FOR EVERY VISITOR.

DAISY - AND HER MASTER, ROBERT, TOOK US ON A TOUR OF THE FRENCH QUARTER DOWN THE STREETS WHERE JAZZ WAS BORN.

New Orleans. We arrived on 4 July – America's Independence Day – and joined in the celebrations.

A WATER HYDRANT PUTTING ON A HAPPY FACE - THE HYDRANTS WERE PAINTED TO CELEBRATE THE 200TH ANNIVERSARY OF AMERICA'S INDEPENDENCE.

TODAY MILLIONS OF JAZZ FANS FLOCK HERE TO HEAR THEIR FAVOURITE MUSIC BEING PLAYED

MOUNT VERNON. THE BEAUTIFUL HOME OF GEORGE WASHINGTON - THE FIRST PRESIDENT OF THE USA

THE LINCOLN MEMORIAL WAS BUILT IN HONOUR OF ABRAHAM LINCOLN WHO WAS PRESIDENT DURING THE BLOODY AMERICAN CIVIL WAR.

Washington The seat of the United States Government. The most famous house in the city is the White House – home of America's President.

Hollywood – Home of the Movies
Multi-million-dollar film star "Jaws" comes in for the attack every five minutes on this tour of Universal Studios.

WATT TOWERS - THESE STRANGE TOWERS ARE THE WORK OF ONE MAN - SIMON ROIRA - WHO BUILT THEM OUT OF ODD BITS OF BROKEN CROCKERY, BOTTLES AND SHELLS, ALL STUCK TOGETHER WITH CEMENT

AT MANNS CHINESE THEATRE WHERE FILM STARS SET THEIR FOOT AND HANDPRINTS IN CONCRETE. THESE WERE THE PRINTS OF THE ROBOTS IN STAR WARS

UP AND OVER...TEXAN STYLE

Houston's "Greased Lightning" roller coaster ride is an experience I'll never forget!

The acceleration at the start of the ride is phenomenal – in just four seconds, you're doing 60 mph. Then you hit the loop. As you enter it, there's a force of 6 G on your body (that meant I weighed 69 stone instead of my normal 11½!

I opened my eyes at the top of the loop for a split second to see the world upside down, before plunging down the other side and up a near-vertical ramp. Then we began going *backwards* – through the loop again – only this time I couldn't see it coming!

No wonder my face is blured in the picture above (that's me on the right) – it was taken at 80 mph!

Space City, – USA is Houston's nickname. It's the Texan home of the NASA Johnson Space Center, which contains America's space shots. The city is space-aged too, with ultra modern skyscrapers everywhere. Everything is air conditioned to make offices, houses and even cars, cool and comfortable because even late in the afternoon, the temperature can be nearing 100°F. You don't even have to go outside to walk from one office block to another. Houston is like a rabbit warren with dozens of tunnels underneath it. More and more are being built, so that eventually you'll be able to walk for 19 miles without ever seeing daylight.

Everything about Houston is big – one shopping centre has 300 shops and two hotels with an ice rink right in the middle. But of all the super modern buildings, there's one that even the Texans call the "Eighth Wonder of the World" – the Houston Astrodome.

When it was opened in 1965, it was the world's first fully air-conditioned indoor arena, big enough to hold baseball and football matches, rodeos, motor-cycle races and polo!

I found the Astrodome a mind-boggling experience. The guide book reads like the *Guinness Book of Records!* The roof is higher than an 18-storey building. Two thousand floodlights blaze down on the 4-acre pitch, using enough electricity to power a city of 9000

Houston's 8th Wonder of the World – the Astrodome – home of the local baseball team, the Astros, where 66000 people can sit in comfort.

people – and 66,000 plush theatre seats surround it. Originally, the turf on the pitch was real, but part of the glass roof had to be painted over to stop the sun glaring into the players' eyes. This killed the grass, so a new playing surface was invented – Astroturf. It's made of nylon and laid like carpet, and can be taken up for sports that don't need a grassy surface. The first Astroturf lasted 12 years. Even then it wasn't thrown away, but cut into 10 cm squares and sold to visitors! I found the scoreboard the most impressive thing in the stadium. It cost one million pounds and has over 50,000 lights. Cowboys appear shooting across the 360′ scoreboard – snarling bulls stampede from side to side – fireworks explode – signs like "Charge" and "Goal" light up – "Happy Birthday" messages flash on, and team information is given in detail.

I stayed to watch the Houston "Astros" baseball team play their match of the season against Los Angeles Dodgers – one of America's top sides.

Britain on a rare, cloudless day – photographed from orbiting Skylab.

Sport in America is an entertainment for all the family. Mascots ran round the pitch, bands and slogans blared from the loudspeakers, urging the crowds to support the Astros. As I watched, I couldn't help thinking how a stadium like the Astrodome would help British football clubs. No more rained off matches, frozen grounds, or frozen spectators!

The highlight of my visit was meeting Astronaut Owen Garriott at the **Johnson Space Center**. He showed me a full-size mock up of America's orbiting space laboratory, "Skylab". The size of the Space Station astounded me. It was 36 metres long and weighed nearly 200,000 lbs.

There were three missions to Skylab, and each had three astronauts living and working in space. Owen Garriott's was the second mission.

The size of the Saturn V rockets is staggering. It was one of these rockets that sent men on their way to the Moon.

It was from this seat that the Skylab Flight Director controlled the 3 space missions.

Skylab was the world's first orbiting laboratory.

Astronaut Owen Garriott spent 59 days in orbit.

America's latest space venture – the Shuttle. This craft will ferry astronauts and scientists to and from orbiting laboratories. First launch date – late 1979.

He showed me the ward room where the astronauts ate their meals and explained how each man chose his own menu on earth before blast off.

The food was dehydrated, so all the astronauts had to do was add water and heat it up. I asked Owen if eating in space was difficult. He told me food that had water added was easy to eat because it was "sticky" and wouldn't float around in the no-gravity atmosphere. But they had to be careful when eating things like peanuts! One at a time was the rule as they couldn't risk a stray peanut getting into the works!

One of the main experiments on the mission was to see how the human body reacted to a long time in space, so the amount of food and drink was measured and all the body wastes collected and sent back to earth for analysis.

In the orbital workshop above the ward room Owen showed me some of the equipment used in experiments. Studying the sun through solar telescopes was an important part of their work. So was photographing the earth. 39000 photographs were taken, including one of Britain on a rare, cloudless day!

I felt very privileged to have been shown round Skylab by someone who'd spent 59 days in space. I wondered whether Owen's space travels were over.

He said: "I'm hoping to fly America's latest spacecraft, the shuttle, when it goes into service late in 1979."

I'm keeping my fingers crossed for him. Watch this space!

Can you solve this case? Six careless mistakes gave away the crook. We spotted them – can you?

THE CASE OF THE
CHINESE TREASURE

The sleek speedboat scudded through the waters of the South China Sea, and ex-Police Superintendent McCann loosened his tie and relaxed.

"How do you like Hong Kong?" he asked his nephew, Bob, who sat beside him, keeping a watchful eye on his set of scuba diving equipment

Bob grinned. "Great! I'm really glad you asked me to come with you on this trip."

"I need someone who knows about diving," said McCann. "You fit the bill. And now I'm a private detective, I decide who works for me."

A slim figure, immaculately dressed in white, sat at the controls of the speeding boat: Dave Ha Giv, a quick-witted Chinese man just a few years older than Bob, and personal assistant to the famous adventurer Sir John Cousins. He asked McCann: "No regrets about leaving the police, then, Mr McCann?"

"Being a private detective means I can do jobs like this one," said McCann simply. "But let's run over the main facts of the case again. Bob."

McCann sat back in his seat, eyes half-closed, fingertips together thoughtfully, as Bob went over the main points yet again.

'Treasure," he began. "Believed to be worth at least a million pounds. Probably the plunder of one of the pirate ships that used to plague this coast. Found by a fisherman. Sir John Cousins, an expert on Chinese history, landed the job of salvaging the stuff. But everyone is dead worried someone will sneak in and whip the treasure from under

his nose ... so Sir John called in Britain's top detective. That way, no one could say he hadn't done his best."

Dave butted in: "That's about the size of it, Mr McCann. You're one of the world's most famous crime-busters. If you can't stop the treasure getting stolen, then no one can."

McCann looked grim. "Why not call in one of the local men – or the official police force?"

Dave looked mysterious. "No more than a dozen people know about the sunken fortune. The fewer people that know, the happier Sir John is. And there have been a couple of daring robberies in Hong Kong lately. The man behind them, an Australian called Bossman Ted, is said to be a brilliant actor who can fool police into giving him information. We don't want to take risks on a job this size!"

"Oh, I've read the file on Bossman Ted," said McCann, thoughtfully. "A slippery customer and no mistake. But tell me about your boss – Sir John Cousins."

Dave turned round in the driver's seat and grinned. "Sticko's a good sort," he said. "A very correct Britisher, you know."

"Sticko?" queried Bob.

"Got a lump of shrapnel in his left leg when he was in the war and always walks with a stick. He's very funny

about it – he used to be a bit of a judo ace. Both of us are very keen on the martial arts. He always says that if his left leg was sound, he'd beat me any day.

But he's a worried man, right now. If that map which marks the site of the treasure gets into the wrong hands, we've lost a million pounds."

Bob whistled: "A pretty pricey scrap of paper!"

Dave nodded agreement as he gunned the engine mightily and eased it towards a remote jetty on one of Hong Kong's green and beautiful outlying islands. Moored at the long, wooden jetty was a single, delapidated fishing junk. Dave smiled at Bob's look of astonishment:

"If we go out to the treasure in a de-luxe schooner, someone just might wonder what we were up to, and then what would happen to our treasure? What better disguise than this leaky old boat?"

"You'd make a good copper," commented McCann as they stepped onto the jetty.

"Look," said Dave. "I'm going out onto the headland to look through the binoculars and see if there's anything suspicious going on. You can't be too careful. Sir John's on the junk, just step aboard and introduce yourselves." So saying, he strode off down the jetty, while McCann and Bob clambered onto the junk and called out:

"Ahoy, there!"

A gruff voice called: "Come aboard!"

Sir John sat in a low-ceilinged, dingy cabin, his right leg propped on a stool, a magnificent mane of white hair swept back from a commanding, honest soldier's face. "Forgive me if I don't get up," he said. "This gammy leg, you know."

They shook hands all round. "Howde do, McCann. And you, you're the diving expert, eh? Capital, capital. But lookee here, both of you. You see this map?" He banged his finger down on a neat red X just off the northern tip of the island. "This piece of paper is worth a million pounds. Get me?"

They both nodded solemnly. "Well, that's that then," said Sir John. "How do you like Hong Kong, eh?"

"Nice and warm after England, sir," said Bob.

"Hmm. I like to get back to the old country every couple of years. Like to see my grandchildren, watch the television with them. They love *Blue Peter* and that Noel Edmonds who runs the show. But the weather back in Blighty is frightful. I'll swear my teeth were chattering when I received my knighthood at Alexandra Palace. Anyway, I expect my man's told you some of the problems about the job."

"That's right," agreed Bob.

"Good, good. Capital chap, my man. Red belt karate fellow – absolutely one of the top men in the world. Anyway, the thing is, we've got to watch the treasure. Funny to think

it's been lying there unguarded since Hong Kong was the capital of all China."

"Well, I'll go and fetch my diving kit," offered Bob.

"Good-oh, sport," said Sir John. "I'll take a turn on the jetty myself."

"Not so fast, Ted," rasped McCann. "You're nicked."

But the awkward figure suddenly took off with lightning speed and his whirling stick caught McCann a sickening blow as the ace detective moved in.

"After him, Bob," rasped McCann as the man took flight and leapt onto the jetty with uncanny agility. But there was no need for Bob to move. A slim, white figure at the far end of the jetty was galvanised into action, sprinting straight for the fleeing figure who tried desperately to swerve.

But escape was impossible as Dave Ha Giv leapt into the air to fell the

phoney Sir John in the most devastating burst of kung-fu action Bob had ever seen. As the fake knight fell, his distinguished mane of hair flopped onto the jetty beside him: a wig.

McCann searched the junk and soon found the gagged and bound figure of the real Sir John. "Thank you. Thank you a thousand times. If he'd got away with that map . . . "

"Bossman Ted would have been a very rich man indeed," completed Bob.

"But how did you get onto him?" gasped Sir John.

"You know my methods, Bob," said McCann.

Bob grinned. "He made six very foolish mistakes."

McCann said wryly: "That's right, Bob. And I think that's the closest the Aussie interloper will ever get to a knighthood!"

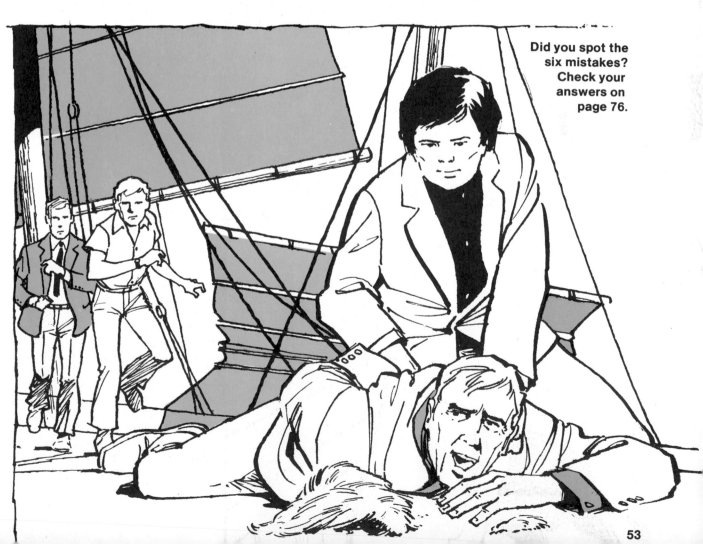

Did you spot the six mistakes? Check your answers on page 76.

In my first year on Blue Peter, I travelled to America and Tanzania, learnt to water ski, had a custard pie thrown in my face, acted the part of an Eskimo, and survived a night in the freezing Bavarian mountains. But it was the Death Slide off Tower Bridge that gave me the most butterflies in my stomach.

It happened when the 45 Commando Group of the Royal Marines from Arbroath, Scotland, invited me to join them on an exercise. The Death Slide is their way of getting men and equipment down cliffs or tall buildings by stretching a rope from the highest point to the ground, and then sliding down it. 72.5-metre-high Tower Bridge was ideal for a training session.

DEATH SLIDE

The ride down the 150-metre rope, slung from a balcony on one of the bridge's twin towers to the opposite bank, would take about thirteen seconds. The expert Marines can slide down at 40 m.p.h. in all kinds of positions. To stop them crashing, a second rope was fixed on a slip ring. Company Sergeant Macdonald, known to his mates as Tosh, was in charge of this. He explained that when I reached the part on the rope where his rope started, it would be a case of his weight breaking my slide. I was glad to see he was a big fellow!

Captain David Nicholls gave me my final briefing. The strap was dunked in water to reduce the friction and stop the rope burning, then I tested the hand loops. David showed me how to sit on the balcony. I just hoped my nerves weren't showing too much!

My heart was thumping as I got into position. There was no turning back now. I inched my way forward, and with a lurch, I was off.

The wind rushed at me. I could feel myself accelerating. My fear left me; the excitement of the ride took over.

At the bottom, I was met by a blaze of flash guns; photographers surrounded me, clicking away.

I felt on top of the world. The press wanted to know if I'd do it again."Yes," I replied . . . and did, two more times!

It's quite a strain on the arms, and three times was enough for safety. For the sheer thrill, the Death Slide and the *Greased Lightning* loop-the-loop roller-coaster ride in Houston come about equal.

To top it all, at the end of the day, I was presented with a Marines Green beret. I felt very honoured – it's something I'll treasure all my life!

400

MEDI-BIKE

350
300
250
200
150
100
75
50
25

We won't forget 1979 in a hurry! Out of 120,000 entries for our International Year of the Child First Day Cover Competition, five-year-old Adrian Cresswell's design was chosen for the official Post Office Cover. Adrian's train, with people of all nationalities waving from the carriages, symbolised world-wide friendship, as did many of the entries.

But before that, our 1979 Medi-Bike Appeal had got the International Year of the Child off to a flying start.

The idea of the Year was that countries all over the world should help children in need, and so many Blue Peter viewers wanted to join in, we did some research.

The results were a dreadful shock! These are some of the statistics given to us by the United Nations:

One-sixth of the babies born each year are underweight and 95% of these are in the developing countries.

Up to one third of all children born alive die from malnutrition and diseases before they are five years old.

Of the ones that survive between a quarter and half suffer from severe malnutrition in the poorest countries.

Even if you have no pocket money, or your father's unlucky enough to be unemployed, it's hard to imagine what it's like to live in one of the *really* poor countries of the world.

Mind you, you wouldn't live for long. In Tanzania, for example, out of every thousand babies born, over a hundred die before they're one year old, and grown-ups are lucky if they live longer than 42 years.

When I took Blue Peter film cameras to Tanzania, Dr Tony Klouda explained the problems. The biggest were the size of the country – about five times as large as the British Isles – the scattered villages, and the lack of proper roads. There was a good scheme of a network of clinics operating from the main hospitals – and a series of dispensaries branching out from the clinics. But the Health Workers taking their

Dr Tony Klouda introduced me to Sajali – the bike repair man.

Abdulla was one of the few Health Workers with transport.

His bike enabled him to treat ten times the number of patients on each visit.

medical kits from the dispensaries to the villages had an impossible task.

"They can't use trucks or cars," Tony said. "There are often only rough tracks leading to the remote villages."

"What do they do?" I asked.

"Walk!" replied Tony.

It was true. The Health Workers were having to walk anything up to eight or nine miles to the villages with their kits and then walk all the way back to their dispensaries *before* nightfall.

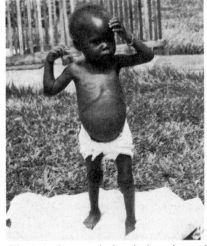
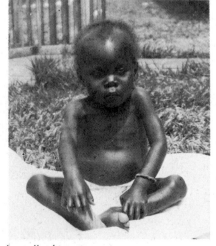

Maria before and after being given vital medical treatment.

"This means they can only see one or two mothers and babies at a time," said Tony.

"No wonder many of the patients don't get proper treatment."

But Abdulla was lucky. He was one of the few Health Workers with transport – a good old trusty bicycle! Tony said the heavy duty bike – tough enough to take all the bumping over the grass and rough tracks – enabled Abdulla to treat ten times the number of patients on each visit.

"The trouble is, bikes are expensive luxuries in Tanzania," he explained. "Only a few Health Workers have them. We need as many as we can get to help all the expectant mothers, babies and small children who are lacking proper medical care."

Who would have thought something as simple as a bike could have been a life saver! We worked out that if only we could provide 400 bikes, complete with medical kits, an extra 2500 babies and children would benefit.

And we also discovered we could provide the Medi-Bikes by collecting used postage stamps and foreign and pre-decimal coins. Amazingly, we reached our target within four weeks – in fact, we were able to make this stupendous announcement on the very first day of the International Year of the Child – 1 January 1979.

The first of our Medi-Bikes – strong and sturdy to withstand wear and tear.

But beating the target was just the beginning! With one of the biggest-ever responses to a Blue Peter Appeal, your stamps and coins came pouring in to the Depot. By the beginning of May we'd been able to provide almost *one thousand* Medi-Bikes.

Tony was overjoyed.

But there was even better news to come. The Government launched a "pound for pound" scheme especially for the International Year of the Child, and promised to double any donations raised for Third World countries like Tanzania. That meant we were able to provide extra help in the shape of badly-needed vaccines and medicines.

And after our Medi-Bike Appeal Auction held by Phillips on 25 May (which raised a record sum for a Blue Peter Sale – £21,558.00) we were able to reach the one-thousand Medi-Bike mark and send additional First Aid supplies for the Health Workers – a tremendous contribution towards the International Year of the Child.

1 January 1979 – we reached our target of 400 Medi-Bikes

Take Hart if you want to draw our Blue Peter Ship!

Tony Hart designed the ship back in 1963. Since then it's appeared on well over a million badges! Here's Tony's ingenious method of drawing our symbol.

First make a collection of circular objects like cups, saucers, lids, jars and coins so you have a good variety of sizes.

These are the sails →

Now practise drawing round the shapes to make overlapping circles; these will give the different types of sail.

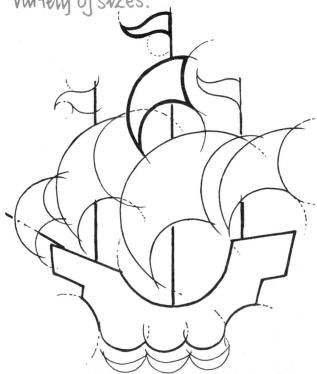

Start your ship by drawing three masts and then using the different objects to draw in the sails.

Colour the ship with paint, crayons or felt tipped pens, or leave it as a silhouette. Good luck!

Tony Hart

The Tale of the Red Indian Princess

Outside St George's Church at Gravesend, 24 miles from London, there stands a statue of a Red Indian princess. She was born in North America, five thousand miles away, more than 370 years ago. What, you may ask, is the statue of a Red Indian princess doing in a graveyard east of London? The answer lies in a strange story which took us on the trail of Princess Pocahontas.

1 On 26 April 1607 three English ships ended a voyage of five thousand miles, and drew near the American shore of Virginia.

2 The men and women began to build houses and a church for they intended to settle here in the New World. They called their new home Jamestown, after King James of England and Scotland. A group of Red Indian children watched them.

3 Their leader was called Pocahontas, and she was the 10-year-old daughter of their Great Chief Powhatan. She made friends with Captain John Smith, and soon she could say in English, "I am your friend."

4 Chief Powhatan and his braves were not so friendly, and they decided to have nothing to do with the English settlers, even when they had a poor harvest and were short of food.

5 Captain Smith bravely led an expedition into the heart of Indian country, to try to buy food. They were set upon by hostile Indians and captured.

6 After a feast in the Red Indian Village, Captain Smith was forced to kneel down and the Indians made ready to club him to death. Suddenly, Princess Pocahontas rushed forward. "He is my friend," she cried. "If you want to kill him, you must kill me first."

7 Chief Powhatan always called Pocahontas "his dear darling daughter", and he could refuse her nothing. John Smith was released, and the Indians promised to trade with them. For a while the English and the Red Indians lived at peace together.

8 Then Captain Smith went back to England, and war broke out. The new governor of Jamestown had Pocahontas, now a beautiful young girl, kidnapped and brought before him. He wanted to exchange her for English prisoners in Indian hands.

9 Pocahontas was handed over to a clergyman and his family. They were very kind to her, even when Powhatan sent word he would not give up his prisoners.

10 Her new family taught her more English, and all about the Christian religion. After a while she was baptised and took a new name – Rebecca.

11 An English settler named John Rolfe admired the beautiful 17-year-old. He wrote a letter to the Head of the settlers in Viginia, saying he would like to marry her. "My hearty and best thoughts are entangled with her," he wrote. "If I marry her it will be for the good of this plantation, for the honour of our country, for the glory of God."

12 So they were married – Pocahontas wore a dress the people of Jamestown had had sent out from England, and a pearl necklace Powhatan gave her. He was not there, but he sent two of his sons to be with his daughter. Everyone was very happy about the marriage.

13 The Indian Princess was very happy as the wife of John Rolfe and they had a son called Thomas. Then, one day they were invited to England to tell important people about the settlement in Virginia.

14 In London, everyone was very interested in Pocahontas, and she was invited to Court, to see King James and Queen Anne. She loved England, but the damp, foggy climate did not agree with her.

15 She fell ill and John Rolfe was glad when it was time to take her back to Virginia. As they waited for the ship, she grew worse. "Do not grieve – we must all die," she said to her husband. "It is enough that the child lives."

Pocahontas died far from home, when she was only twenty years old. Her son Thomas lived, and went to live in Virginia. In the United States today, many people are proud to say they are descended from him, and from Princess Pocahontas. And ten years ago, the Governor of Virginia gave the statue that stands at Gravesend – where she died – in memory of the Red Indian princess who longed to see peace for all time between the Red Indians and the White Men.

♪ Tiddle im pom pom ♪

That's how the Blue Peter opening signature tune's known in the BBC Its proper title is *Barnacle Bill,* and the same recording was used for over twenty years – until Simon met Mike Oldfield, one of Britain's top instrumentalists and composers. His *Tubular Bells,* in which he played just about every instrument, has sold over 9 million copies around the world.

Mike offered to give his special treatment to our tune in his home recording studio. He uses a 24-track tape recorder, so that he can record each instrument he plays separately on a different track, then he mixes all the sounds together, he can adjust the volume and quality of each instrument individually.

Track 1: He recorded a "tick tock" sound to give himself the rhythm of the tune. This wouldn't be heard on the final version, but it would guarantee that every instrument he played would be at the same speed.

Track 2: An acoustic guitar would give the basic rhythm sound.

Tracks 3, 4, 5 & 6: Mike played a Bodhran – an Irish drum. He recorded this twice. Then he hit the studs on the drum to give a metallic sound. Again, this was recorded twice.

Tracks 7, 8 & 9: Synthesisers are electronic gadgets that can produce sounds from explosions to organs. Mike used several. On this one he played the melody of our tune.

Tracks 10 & 11: The film crew joined in playing an assortment of bells.

Track 12, 13 & 14: Mike's an expert guitarist – here he's playing an electric guitar to add a bit of "rock & roll"! He recorded a track with an acoustic bass too!

Tracks 15 & 16: The opening drum roll was played by someone who's always wanted to be a rock drummer!

Mixing the sounds together.
Mike's a perfectionist! It took over an hour to mix just 1½ minutes of music.

Mike's version of *Barnacle Bill* was an instant hit with Blue Peter viewers, so we asked him if we could use it all the time.

"Delighted," he said. "I'll do the closing music as well, if you like."

Naturally, we were thrilled to bits. Mike's version has given "Tiddle im pom pom" a brand new lease of life!

How can a limerick cause an explosion?

By winning a Blue Peter Competition

There were over 6000 entries for the Goldie Limerick competition. The contestants had to supply the last three lines of a limerick which began:
There was a young dog on Blue Peter
Whose nature could not have been sweeter . . .

The three winners – one for each age group – were given the chance to blow up a chimney. Not all by themselves, you understand! We didn't just give them a bag of gelignite, point to the nearest chimney and tell them to get on with it. No, the winners were brought from their homes at Selly Oak, near Birmingham, Charlton-cum-Hardy, near Manchester, and Belfast in Northern Ireland to Peterborough, where demolition expert George Williams had five chimneys primed and detonated, ready at the touch of a button to be blown to smithereens. At least, that's what we thought at the time. But more of that later . . .

The chimneys were all that remained of what used to be a flourishing brickworks back in 1898. Now, where once teams of horses pulled carts piled high with fresh, red bricks straight from the kilns, there was nothing but a bleak wasteland of rubble with the chimneys standing like stubborn gravestones to a long dead age.

Now even *they* had to go, and George Williams, who last year helped me to break a world record by blowing up ten chimneys at once, decided to give Blue Peter viewers the fun of pressing the button.

Chris, Lesley and Goldie with the top prize winners, Sian Meyrick, Rodney Moffitt and Emma Jayne Corless.

65

The first to go was 12-year-old Sian Meyrick from Selly Oak. George had already run out the cable and all that remained was for Sian, looking quite apprehensive in her tin hat, to press the button.

I asked George if the 50-m.p.h. wind which was driving clouds of dust into our faces was going to give him problems.

"No, I don't think so." He screwed up his face in the wind and looked towards the chimney. "Their weight should carry them down."

He crouched down and wound up the charge which primes the exploder ready to fire.

I asked Sian if she'd like to recite her prize-winning limerick for the last time before pressing the button.

"There was a young dog on Blue Peter
 Whose nature could not have been sweeter.
 While listening to stereo
 She sings oh so merry-o,
 But is rather more woofer than tweeter."

"O.K. 5, 4, 3, 2, 1 – Blow!"

Her thumb hit the button and immediately there was the roar of the explosion and a huge cloud of smoke and dust enveloped the chimney. And then . . . silence. Nothing but the wind blowing dust into our eyes. It cleared. And there, to our utter astonishment, was revealed 160 feet of chimney standing like a sentry, wounded but refusing to fall.

I've never been more at a loss for words in my life. It was so quiet I could even hear the low purr of the motor on the Blue Peter cameras. At last I managed –

"What do you think, George?" which was a fairly banal remark in the circumstances. George raised his eyes to heaven and said:

"Disgusting!"

I felt so sorry for him. He had, in his lifetime, successfully detonated more than 200 chimneys. It was his first failure and he had to make it in front of 8,000,000 people!

Never mind – if at first you don't succeed, you lay another charge and try again.

"5, 4, 3, 2, 1."

This time there was no mistake. The base of the chimney was blown clean away – and although she remained defiantly suspended for a fraction of a second, slowly and sedately, with a crescendo of a roar, she gave up the ghost.

The next demolisher was 9-year-old Emma Jayne Corless from Chorlton-cum-Hardy, whose winning entry was:

"There was a young dog on Blue Peter
 Whose nature could not have been sweeter.
 When asked to appear
 She said 'All right, my dear,
 I might collar the lead in *Evita*.'"

Emma had two chimneys to blow and George felt confident that this time it was going to be all right. But the Blue Peter cameraman was getting worried about the light. It had taken a long time to recharge Sian's chimney, and by now we were well into the bleak December afternoon with darkness already beginning to loom. George and his team were carefully laying the explosives at the foot of the chimneys, and then running out the cable to connect it to the exploder. Even when the light is failing, there's no point in trying to hurry a man in charge of an explosion.

Emma, however, was full of confidence as George started the countdown in the twilight.

"5, 4, 3, 2, 1." Boom!

The far chimney leapt off its base and neatly cascaded into a pile of bricks. The near one seemed to teeter, like an old lady about to fall who somehow miraculously regains her balance and then seems to stand up straighter than ever.

It was held up by the wind and half a dozen bricks.

George and I were totally speechless, but Emma looked on the bright side.

George packs the explosive into holes at the chimney's base.

The winners draw straws to decide who goes first.

"It's getting better, though, isn't it?" she said, laying a sympathetic hand on George's shoulder.

There was nothing to do but run out the cable and try again. We all held our breath whilst George and the men approached the chimney, which we knew was hanging on by a thread, and given a good gust of wind could collapse at any minute.

At last George, now showing signs of strain, reported that all was ready for another attempt. Then, to everybody's intense relief, the last few bricks were blown away – and down she came.

By now it was 5 o'clock and pitch dark. The Blue Peter cameraman's worry about the light had turned to despair and battery lights were produced to light up the small, sleepy figure of 6-year-old Rodney Moffitt from Belfast. Rodney had been up since 5 o'clock that morning to start his long journey from Ireland, and by the time we were ready to go, he was ready for bed.

"There was a young dog on Blue Peter,
Whose nature could not have been sweeter.
'I'm Goldie,' she whined,
'Not as smart as K9,
But I do think my coat is much neater.'"

He stifled a yawn and pressed the button.

The inky landscape was lit up by a flash of white light, and for an instant we could seen Rodney's chimney standing erect. Then it was velvet black again, but out of the darkness came a roar of falling bricks which brought smiles of relief to all our faces. Rodney's explosion had been the best of the lot.

"Oh well done, Rodney," said George with undisguised enthusiasm.

"I'll bet you liked that, didn't you?" I said. Rodney tried to smile, but this time the yawn won. It summed up all our feelings. It had been a long, cold, frustrating day. But in the end, it was a happy one.

We all crouch down as the countdown begins, but nothing happens and George has to set the charge again.

5–4–3–2–1 – boom! This time we were lucky.

Emma's turn and we all held our breath.

Rodney was nearly asleep when his turn came.

Houses where someone famous lived often give you a powerful feeling that the people are still there, in the chairs they sat on, the gardens they strolled in, or in the books they read – or wrote!

Blue Peter Special Assignmen

I went with the Blue Peter Special Assignment Team to houses all over England, France and Italy, and with a group of actors, we went on a journey back through time . . .

1 Marie Antoinette at Versailles

Marie Antoinette was 15 when she arrived at Versailles, the most splendid palace in Europe, from her home in Vienna, to marry a man she had never seen; the grandson of the King of France. Four years later she became Queen, and ruled as Queen of fashion, with 150 new dresses a year. She was a foreigner and the French people hated her and at last she was dragged from Versailles to Paris, where she died on the guillotine.

2 Rudyard Kipling at Bateman's

Kipling and his wife arrived in a veteran car at the house that was to be their home for thirty years. He was famous for his books about India – the *Jungle Books*, the *Just So Stories*, *Kim* – but he loved this house and declared "England is the most marvellous of all foreign countries that I have been in!"

3 St Thérèse of Lisieux

Thérèse Martin lived with her father and big sisters in a house in Lisieux, in Northern France. She made up her mind to give up her whole life to God, and when she was 14 she begged the Pope himself to allow her to enter the Carmelite convent in Lisieux the following year. She lived there until she was 24, and then she died, but the book she had written, *The History of a Soul*, made her so famous that she was proclaimed a saint.

4 The Duke of Wellington at Stratfield Saye

When the Duke of Wellington defeated Napoleon at the Battle of Waterloo, his grateful country gave him money to buy a country estate. He chose Stratfield Saye, 30 miles from London, and settled there with his wife, his two sons, and Copenhagen, the horse he had ridden all day at Waterloo. When Copenhagen died, he was buried in the grounds with military honours. When the Duke was an old man, the 25-year-old Queen Victoria paid him a state visit at Stratfield Saye.

5 The Brontës at Haworth

In 1820, the Reverend Patrick Brontë arrived with his six small children at Haworth which was to be their new home. They were happy at first, reading together at home, or playing on the wide open moors.

They were all to die tragically young, but two of them – Charlotte and Emily – became great writers. Because of them and their books, today everyone knows the name Brontë, and thousands of visitors go to Haworth every year, in their footsteps.

6 Vivaldi in Venice

Red-haired Antonio Vivaldi grew up in his father's barber's shop in Venice. He learned to play the violin and the organ, and to compose. When he grew up, he became a priest, but soon he was made music master in a girls' school and wrote for their orchestra and choir. Vivaldi became very famous, but by the end of his life his music became unfashionable and for two hundred years it was almost unplayed. Yet today, Vivaldi's music is known and loved all over the world.

Tina Heath didn't have a television set until she was 13 years old. But that didn't stop her from becoming a secret tele-addict. Every Monday and Thursday she was late home from school because she went to her friend Janice's house to watch Blue Peter.

In those days, it was Valerie Singleton, Christopher Trace, and a mongrel dog called Petra. I asked Tina if it had crossed her mind that one day she would be taking Valerie's place.

"Not at all. In those days I was going to be a great ballerina!"

By a strange coincidence, when I was 13 years old – I thought I was going to be a ballerina and even more strangely, so did Valerie!

"I went to Drama school and specialised in ballet," Tina went on, "until one day, they told me my feet would never be strong enough, so I decided to be an actress instead. After I left Drama school, I played a lot of small parts on television – until out of the blue, I was asked to audition for the lead in a Children's

Television serial. The only trouble was that "Lizzie Dripping" – that was the name of the part – was supposed to be 12 years old, and I was nearly 20!

"Was that a terrible problem?"

"Well, no – not in the end. I'm about the same height as you – 5 feet – which was a help. By the time I got into a gym slip and put my hair in plaits – everyone said I could have gone for half fare on the buses!"

Tina did two series of *Lizzie Dripping* – until at the age of 22, she thought that she might be pushing her luck to do another year in the first form!

"I seemed to specialise in dying in the following year. I played Helen Burns in *Jane Eyre* and died of consumption – and for my next job, I was machine-gunned to death in *Target*. It was absolutely revolting. I had to wear a special jacket under my dress that was full of holes with little plastic bags of blood behind them. The whole thing was wired up to a detonator which I held in my hand. When I pressed it, every hole exploded and shot out the artificial blood, which looked as though I'd been hit with a hail of bullets. It looked so awful, they had to cut the shot out of the final film, so after all that, I had to die in the distance!"

Tina as Lizzy Dripping with Sonia Dresdel as the 'witch'.

Tina loves to ride. She was brought up in the Wiltshire countryside, which gave her a taste for outdoor life, which still survives, in spite of living in London. The riding became all important when she went up for the part of Rosie in *Black Beauty*.

"The more things you are able to do as an actress, the more opportunities you get. I've always enjoyed swimming, for instance, which was very useful when I was in an episode of *The Sweeney*, because I had to spend the entire time in a swimming pool. I was so long in the water that when I was eventually allowed out, I looked like a piece of corrugated cardboard!"

"You'll find that experience very useful doing this job, too," I said, remembering the time I nearly drowned in Borneo. But I didn't tell her about that. Instead, I asked her, seriously, what worried her most about joining Blue Peter.

"Being myself," she said, without any hesitation. "For the last 10 years, I've been an actress with a character to play, so that most of Tina Heath disappeared. From now onwards, it's going to be ME – plain and unadulterated."

Tina, of course, has already had a go at being herself on television, because she was one of the presenters on *The Sunday Gang* – the religious programme on Sunday mornings..

"That was a great experience in more ways than one. I enjoyed it because I happen to be a Christian – so I believed in what I was doing. And also because there was rather a nice Musical Director, called Dave Cooke, who worked on the show – and 18 months ago, we got married!"

Finally, I asked her what she was most looking forward to about working on Blue Peter.

She thought for a moment, wrinkling her nose – like Lizzie Dripping when she spoke to the witch:

"Meeting all the different people that come on the programme, and having 8,000,000 new friends!"

Good luck, Tina! I hope you'll be as happy as I was on Blue Peter.

Transform your Christmas parcels and crackers and make your table look extra special with these expensive-looking flowers. All you need are scraps of gift ribbon (the kind that sticks to itself when it's moistened), some glue and tinsel.

For the red flowers you need four pieces of ribbon about 8 cm long. Cut the ends into a pointed petal shape, moisten the centre of each strip and give the ribbon one twist in the centre. Press firmly between your finger and thumb to hold the twist in place.

When you have cut and twisted all four pieces, moisten the centre of one of them and put a second piece over it to make a cross.

Add the third and fourth pieces in the same way to make a flower.

Put a dot of glue in the centre and add a small piece of tinsel.
Cut a leaf shape from green ribbon and glue to the back of the flower.

White Christmas Roses are made in the same way, but use rather shorter strips of ribbon and cut the ends rounded rather than pointed. When glueing the flower, press the petals upwards to get the correct shape.

Candle Holder

plasticine →

Bottle top →

Cotton reel →

Cardboard →

Cover with silver foil

ild up clusters of roses to
corate different-sized parcels
d crackers, and individual flowers
n be turned into jewellery by fixing
des or safety pins on the back.

Decorate with roses (keeping them
away from the candle) and *fireproof*
tinsel.

73

TOP TEN BIRDS

Between 8 and 9 o'clock in the morning on Saturday, 27 January 1979 was bird–spotting hour all over the United Kingdom. The Royal Society for the Protection of Birds asked Blue Peter viewers' help to find out how birds were coping with the severe winter in different parts of the country. Over 20,000 spotting reports flooded in, 58 different species of birds were recorded, and from all the information the R.S.P.B. were able to make up a Top Ten Bird Chart.

1 **Starling**
2 **House Sparrow**
3 **Blackbird**
4 **Chaffinch**
5 **Blue Tit**
6 **Robin**
7 **Song Thrush**
8 **Greenfinch**
9 **Great Tit**
10 **Dunnock**

Starling. Over 135,000 sightings. Most common in the South-West.

House Sparrow. Spotted 90,000 times. In the Midlands there was an average of 14 in every garden.

Blackbird. Seen most in Scotland with an average of five in every garden.

Chaffinch. The highest count was in Northern Ireland with an average of six in every garden.

74

Blue Tit. Wales had the most sightings – three in every garden.

Robin – the Christmas card favourite. Again, Wales had the most – two in every garden.

Song Thrush. Two per garden were spotted in the Midlands.

Greenfinch. Seen in twice as many town gardens as country ones, especially in East Anglia where they had two per garden.

Great Tit. Wales were top again with two per garden.

Dunnock, or Hedge Sparrow. Seen more in the country gardens of Scotland and East Anglia with an average of one per garden.

The bad weather forced a lot of birds which normally live in the countryside into gardens where they could find food.

Mainly in Scotland people reported pheasants in their gardens, and in the Isle of Man, 30 curlews were seen by one person. Fieldfares, a type of Thrush, are usually only seen in fields, but they, too, came close to houses in search of food.

Fourteen-year-old Blue Peter viewer Andrew Dodd, from Basildon in Essex, spotted a Waxwing – an occasional visitor from Scandinavia. In Nottingham, the Dakin family had a Great Crested Grebe visit their garden. It had apparently got lost in a blizzard and flown into a telegraph wire. Their vet said that, fortunately, it hadn't been hurt, so after ringing it so that it would be recognised if it was found again, the Dakins released it in a nature reserve.

The most exciting report came from Gloucestershire where Blue Peter viewers, Mr & Mrs Haynes, logged an astonishing 96 wrens roosting

under the roof of their house – by far the greatest number ever recorded in Britain. All the 20,000 reports were of immense value to the R.S.P.B., who want us to say a big thank you to every one who helped on that cold, January morning.

The Dakin family to the rescue.

Great Crested Grebe – got lost in Nottingham.

SOLUTIONS

Puzzle Pictures

1 These four breeds featured on the 1979 British Dog stamps: an Irish Red Setter, an Old English Sheepdog, a Welsh Springer Spaniel and a West Highland Terrier.

2 The heaviest Ted in the world, weighing 18 stone or 114 kilos! His vital statistics are equally colossal – waist 8' 8" (2.64m) and inside leg 4' 4" (1.32m).

3 Members of the Trans-Globe Expedition, including Bothy, the Jack Russell, who came to the studio with all their equipment, including a cardboard house.

4 A "wounded" Simon Groom during a practice Disaster Emergency Exercise at Crystal Palace Railway Station.

5 Seven-year old Toto, the youngest member of Mzumba – the Southern African dance company, Kenny interpreted, as Toto had only just started to learn English.

6 A 50 lb (22.75 kg) Christmas pudding towed by gun carriage into the studio by the officers and men of HMS Heron, the Royal Naval Air Station at Yeovilton.

7 Simon beat Chris to the top of Lesley's boots in the great Blue Peter Button Hook Race.

8 The boys of King's College Choir in their "Etons" – the outfits they wear to and from chapel. Thanks to our S.O.S., the choir received 200 collapsible top hats for their foreign tours, so the tradition of 140 years remains unbroken.

9 This 15-foot (4.60m) long model of Horse Guards Parade is made from 400,000 toy plastic bricks.

10 The world's longest paper chain made in aid of the Multiple Sclerosis Society needed a removal van to carry it away from the studio.

The Case of the Chinese Treasure

1 The real Sir John would have rested his left leg on a stool.

2 Noel Edmonds does not run Blue Peter.

3 The real Sir John would have received his knighthood at Buckingham Palace, not Alexandra Palace.

4 Hong Kong was never the capital of China. Peking is the real capital. As an expert in Chinese history, the real Sir John would have known that.

5 A real martial arts expert would know that a top karate ace would be a black belt, not a red belt.

6 A correct Britisher would not say: "Good-oh, sport!", but an Australian would.

Stick Insects

The number of stick insects in the photograph on page 46 was 14.

USEFUL INFORMATION

Stick Insects:
Don Kennedy, Beautiful Butterflies Ltd., High Street, Bourton-on-the-Water, Glos.

The Evacuees Exhibition:
The Imperial War Museum, Lambeth Road, London SE1. Opening times:
Weekdays – 10.00 – 17.50
Sundays – 14.00 – 17.50

The Tradescant Trust:
7 The Little Boltons, London SW10 9LJ.

Blue Peter Special Assignment:
Kipling's House:
Bateman's, Burwash, Sussex.
Vivaldi's Orphanage:
Ospedale della Pietà, Riva degli Schiavoni, San Marco.

Marie Antoinette's Palace:
Palace of Versailles, Versailles, France.
St Thérèse's House:
Les Buissonets, Lisieux, Calvados, France.
The Brontës' House:
The Parsonage, Haworth, Keighley, Yorkshire.

United States Tourist Board:
24 Grosvenor Square, London W1.

R.S.P.B. & The Young Ornithologists' Club:
The Lodge, Sandy, Bedfordshire.

Buckfast Abbey:
Buckfast, Buckfastleigh, Devon.

BLUE PETER BOOKS

Paddington's Blue Peter Story Book
by Michael Bond, published by Fontana Lion, price 60p.

The Blue Peter Make, Cook & Look Book
By Biddy Baxter, Hazel Gill & Margaret Parnell, published by BBC Publications, £1.50.

The Blue Peter Book of Limericks
Edited by Biddy Baxter & Rosemary Gill, published by Piccolo/BBC, 40p.

Blue Peter Special Assignments
Rome, Paris & Vienna : Venice & Brussels : Madrid, Dublin & York : London, Amsterdam & Edinburgh : by Edward Barnes & Dorothy Smith, published by Severn House, £2.75.

Petra – A Dog for Everyone
By Biddy Baxter & Edward Barnes, published by Pelham Books, £2.95.

Blue Peter Books Nos. 1 – 15
are now out of print, so hang on to your copies, they may become collectors' items!

ACKNOWLEDGEMENTS

Co-ordinator: **Gillian Farnsworth**

Granny's Biscuits, Studio and Christmas Roses by **Margaret Parnell**

Designed by David Playne, assisted by Bob Ayliffe, Chris Norman, Laurie Clark, Lois Wigens, Craig Warwick and Jon Davis.

I Do Not Cry was written by **Dorothy Smith** *The Tale of the Red Indian Princess* and *The Gardening Family* were illustrated by **Robert Broomfield**

ALL PHOTOGRAPHS IN THIS BOOK WERE TAKEN BY

Joan Williams, Michael Cullen, David Clarke, Derek Catani, Peter Lane, David Graem Baker, John Adcock, Christopher Steele-Perkins and Paul Wheeler with the exception of
Giant Teddy by Syndication International;
Evacuees photographs by Radio Times Hulton Picture Library;
Tradescant portraits by the Ashmolean Museum;

Bees by the Slide Centre;
Stick Insects by Beautiful Butterflies Ltd.;
Skylab and Shuttle by NASA;
Maria pictures by Visual Aids (OXFAM);
Chimneys by Keystone Press & Syndication International;
Blackbird, Dunnock & Waxwing by Bruce Coleman Ltd;
Starling, House Sparrow, Chaffinch, Robin, Song Thrush & Greenfinch by Eric Hosking;
Blue Tit and Great Tit by R.S.P.B.

BLUE PETER COMPETITION

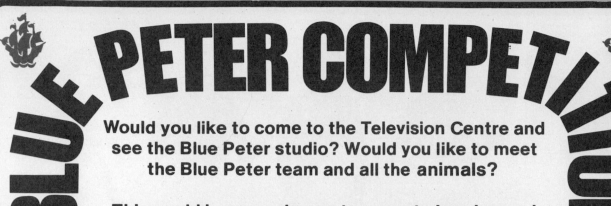

Would you like to come to the Television Centre and see the Blue Peter studio? Would you like to meet the Blue Peter team and all the animals?

This could be your chance to come to London and meet them all at a special party!

This photo of Goldie with Amber and Angus, her mother and father, was taken on her First Birthday. Write not more than three lines telling us what *you* think Angus was saying to Goldie.

The twenty-four people who send us the best suggestions will be invited to our

BLUE PETER PARTY

and there'll be lots of competition badges for the runners-up, too! The closing date: 15 January 1980.

Cut out your entry and send it to:
Blue Peter Competition,
BBC Television Centre,
London W12 7RJ

First prize winners and runners-up will be notified by letter.

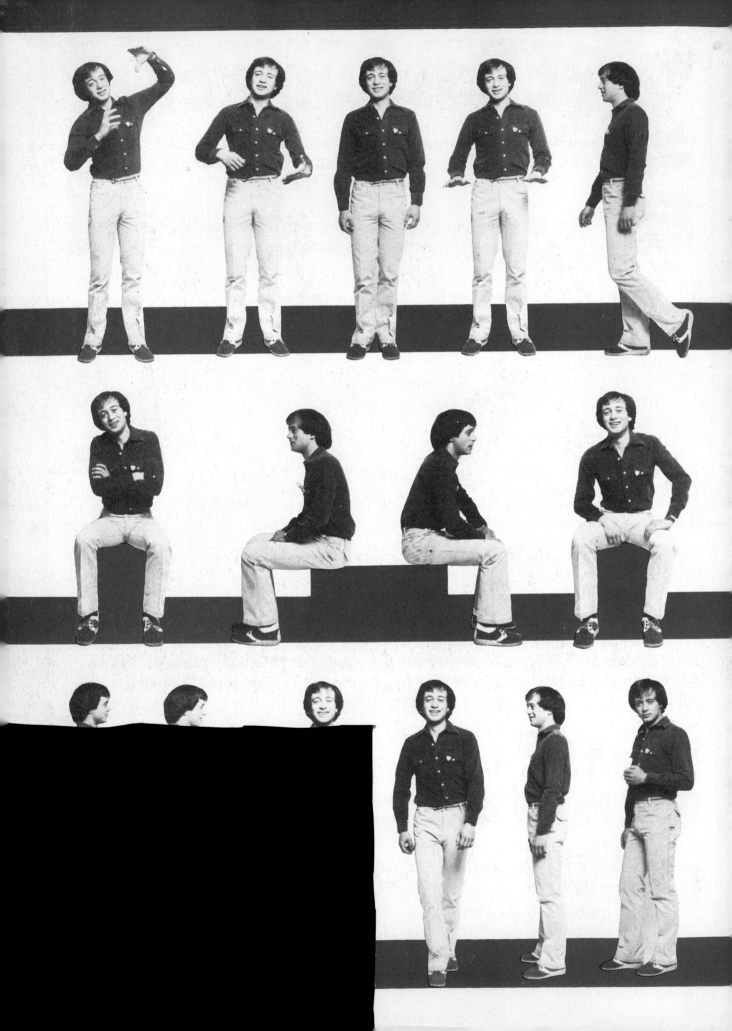